PROPHETIC DESTINY

and the

APOSTOLIC REFORMATION

**A preview to the new book
"Apostles/Prophets &
The Coming Moves of God"**

DR. BILL HAMON

Foreword by PETER WAGNER
Commendation by ORAL ROBERTS

Prophetic Destiny
and the Apostolic Reformation

Copyright © Dr. Bill Hamon, 1996

Produced by:
CHRISTIAN INTERNATIONAL PUBLISHERS
P. O. Box 9000
Santa Rosa Beach, FL 32459

Published by
Forry & Hacker Inc.

All Scriptures are taken from New King James Version (NKJV) except when designated.

CONTENTS

. . . .

Ministries Being Brought Forth to Further Fulfill Malachi 4:5,6
A New Apostolic Reformation?
Some of the Revolutionary Changes Perceived at This Point
Who will be the Leaders in the New Apostolic Reformation?
A Personal Prophetic Vision of the Last Chapter of God's Book of
     His Mortal Church
The Last Chapter - Divine Decrees and New Directives Being
     Made in Heaven
Apostles and Prophets Arising in the World of Administration
     and Finances

The Apostolic Movement/Reformation
Same Purposes as Preceding Five Movements
God's Purpose for the Apostolic Movement
Will Drastically Affect the Church and Nations of the World
The Third World War- Church is Determining Factor
What Is the Apostolic Movement
What it Is Not
Apostle-Prophets & Final Moves of God Chapter Headings

"Behold the Goodness and the Severity of God"
Essentials for Apostles and Prophets

4. The Last Day Ministry of Apostles and Prophets

The days in which we live are not normal times. The extraordinary works of God in every continent of the world have caused me, along with many other leaders, to lift our voices in praise for the supreme privilege of being a Christian in this remarkable generation.

One of the principal figures whom God has been using to shape such a generation of believers is my friend, Bishop Bill Hamon. I must confess that I still feel a sense of awe when I call Bill Hamon a "friend." For years and years he was, for me, a distant Christian celebrity, whose name I knew and heard frequently, whom I greatly admired, and whose books had been among the most influential in nurturing me through what I refer to as my "paradigm shift" from traditional Christianity to an openness to the person and to the full ministry of the Holy Spirit. I never was presumptuous enough to imagine that I would ever meet him personally, much less develop the strong relationship that we now have.

His book, Prophets and Personal Prophecy, was the only book I could find during the 1980's that, to me, made biblical and practical sense of the gift and office of prophet in the church today. My copy is as scratched up, underlined and dog-eared as any book in my library. I have referred to it often in my writings and I recommend it highly to my students.

Bishop Hamon's new book, Apostles & Prophets and The Coming Moves of God, is a thrill to read. It is so timely! God has not been standing still. His purposes and works in the 1990's are not the same as they were in the 1980's. The Holy Spirit continues to speak to the churches, and Bill Hamon is one who has special spiritual ears to hear what He is saying. Just as the 1980's was a decade initiating the renewal of the biblical gift and office of prophet, the 1990's is shaping up to be the decade in which God is renewing the gift and office of apostle.

As a professional in the field of church growth, it has become obvious to me that the fastest growing cutting edge of world wide Christianity in our times is what I like to call the New Apostolic Reformation, previously referred to by some as independent churches or nondenominational churches or postdenominational churches or grass-roots churches or other kinds of names. Whatever the name, the fact of the matter is that we are seeing, before our very eyes, the most radical change in the way of doing Christianity since the Protestant Reformation. The changes are obvious on every continent, and there are many commonalities.

As the name would imply, one of the chief features of the New Apostolic Reformation, setting it apart from the more traditional versions of Christianity, is the emerging recognition of the role of apostles in the Body of Christ. Because this is such a key to advancing the Kingdom of God and because the notion of contemporary apostles is so new to many of us, including myself, an urgent need of our times is wise and recognized leadership by those through whom God has been speaking and working along these lines for some time. Bill Hamon is one whom God has raised up to meet this need. Just as he helped us understand the role of the prophet a decade ago, he now helps us understand the role of apostle today.

As you read this book you will sense an excitement about what God is doing to and through His people. Before you finish, you will not want to be simply a spectator, but you will want to launch out personally into this new stream of the Holy Spirit. You will not find a better navigator for this exhilarating trip than Bill Hamon.

Peter Wagner
Fuller Theological Seminary
Colorado Springs, Colorado

I want to confirm my love for you and confidence in you as you walk in holiness and divine guidance before the Lord. You have a tender heart yet a strong presentation of your knowledge and experience with the use of the ministry gifts of apostles and prophets, how they are linked together, also linked with the 5-fold ministry gifts.

Bill, you are bringing truths that are very much needed to the Body of Christ. The Lord's hand is surely on you. I admire you for being bold, in His name, to what you feel is going to be done through His apostles and prophets in the move of God. I pray that God will multiply your ministry which is so urgently needed today.

Oral Roberts
Oral Roberts University, Tulsa, Oklahoma

INTRODUCTION

· · · · · · · · ·

THIS BOOK HAS A THREE-FOLD PURPOSE:

(1). To Show What is Happening Now in the Church and What Is Next.

Our first objective is to reveal to all saints what the Holy Spirit is seeking to accomplish in this day and hour. Everyone needs to know what is happening in the Church today and how it is working together to fulfill God's ultimate purpose.

(2). To Reveal Insights Concerning The New Apostolic Reformation/Movement.

We want everyone to know that we are in the midst of a major restoration movement. The Prophetic-Apostolic Movements are destined to bring full restoration of the Prophet and Apostle ministries into the Church. The Prophetic Movement has been doing that for the Prophet for several years. Now the Apostolic Movement is doing the same for the Apostle. In the major work on Apostles and Prophets detailed information is given on these movements. In this little book we give the revelation that there is an Apostolic Movement and a birds-eye view of what it is destined to accomplish.

(3). To Reveal Insights Into Fulfilling Your Prophetic Destiny.

Along with the importance of the others is the great need for all those who are called of God to understand the process He takes us through to fulfill our prophetic destiny. Since the Prophetic Movement has produced a great company of prophets, thousands of Christians are receiving personal prophecies confirming and revealing fivefold callings and membership ministries in Christ's Church. It is essential especially for those receiving the calling of prophet or apostle for them to understand the long period and process between one's calling and commissioning. Someday I will expand that truth into a book of its own.

It is so vital that those called to fulfill a particular membership ministry in the Body of Christ know the divine process that takes a person from their calling to their commissioning to that ministry.

The greater the calling of responsible ministry in the Body of Christ the greater the intensity and length of the process. This is especially true of those called to be prophets and apostles. It is also true of those called to be national and international leaders in God's kingdom. Many in the Bible and throughout the Church Age have failed to fulfill their destiny. I believe often it was because they did not have a clear understanding of God's process for preparing them for that great ministry.

I pray that this book will be a blessing to all who read it. May we all have ears to hear what the Holy Spirit wants to say to us from what has been written in these pages. We have used the Foreword by Dr. Peter Wagner and one commendation from the many I received from major Church leaders around the world. All of the commendations are in the new book, which is about 300 pages, titled *"Apostles/Prophets and The Coming Moves of God."*

1

WHAT IS
HAPPENING NOW?

. . . .

The kingdom prayer of Jesus is in its last stages of fulfillment. "Thy kingdom come, Thy will be done on earth as it is in Heaven." His kingdom is being established first in the Church. We are to give Him the full domain as King and Lord of our lives. The Refreshing Revival is activating our first love for our King Jesus and His personal presence. The Apostolic Movement/Reformation will release the powerful domain of the King. When we allow the King to take His rightful domain within us then His powerful dominion works will be manifested through us.

Holiness and Righteousness are Being Laid to God's Plumb Line. The wind of God is blowing over the Church for more purposes than blessing and refreshing. The Holy Spirit has now been commissioned to start **separating** the **chaff** from the **wheat**, **profane** from **pure**, **flesh** from **Spirit**, and the **false** from the **true.** God will be purifying the inward life and prophetic flow of the prophets and the apostles by separating man's religious ideas from heaven's pure words. He will be separating **self-activated actions** from **Holy Spirit manifestations, self-serving ministry** from **sacrificial ministry, personal kingdom ministry** from **God's kingdom**. The present truth Church will no longer be a mixed multitude but a disciplined army under dominion. It will be like the time of Israel after three months of sovereign deliverance from Egypt and supernatural manifestations such as the Red Sea being rolled back, healing at Marah and manna falling daily from Heaven. They had to make the transition of being separated into tribes, put in divine order around the Tabernacle, and everyone given direction and designation for their area of responsibility and ministry. During the first phase of God's great move they were a mixed multitude. They were joyful in their deliverance, signs, wonders and God supernaturally supplying for all their needs. But they were wandering aimlessly without knowing what was coming next, what part they were to play or what God's progressive purpose was in all that was happening.

Now is the time of God's people camping around the Mountain of God until everyone knows their calling, placement, ministry and relationship to God's greater purpose within His local and universal Church. There are to be no more mixtures of flesh and Spirit in a person or prophetic flow. God is separating and calling His Church to come out of the Egyptian/Babylonian religious system to know their calling and membership ministry in God's spiritual Body of Christ, the Church.

A Restorational Move of God vs. A Holy Spirit Refreshing and Renewal. There is a different purpose for each of these divine visitations. A restoration movement is when God sovereignly chooses to restore certain major truths, ministries and spiritual experiences that have not been active since the early years of the Church. Holy Spirit renewal or refreshing is when God sends His refreshing spiritual rain to prepare His people for the next restorational move of God. These Holy Spirit moves are usually referred to as revivals, such as the Welsh Revival. It is called a "Renewal" when the Holy Spirit blows into every church denomination to update them into all presently restored truths, ministries and spiritual experiences, such as the Charismatic Renewal. Holy Spirit Refreshings and Renewals do not restore major truths or ministries to the corporate Church, but they do bring supernatural spiritual experiences into the lives of individual believers. Revivals, refreshings and renewals happen every so often in the Church, often just before a restorational movement.

The Holy Spirit is presently taking the Church through a process of transition, preparation and progression toward the Apostolic Movement and final restorational moves of God. All who are presently participating in the refreshing revival must maintain their joy, deliverance, and divine transformation. While at the same time proper response must be made to the Holy Spirit's challenge to be established in all the restorational realities that God has restored in the Prophetic and will restore in the Apostolic Movement.

Ministries Being Brought Forth to Further Fulfill Malachi 4:5,6.

The Promise Keepers ministry was born of the Holy Spirit to further fulfill God's prophetic purpose stated in Malachi. They are turning the hearts of men of all ages to God. This is causing the "hearts of the fathers to turn to the children and the hearts of the children to turn to the fathers."

The Generals of Intercession ministry directed by Cindy Jacobs is also a part of the fulfillment of this prophecy. Cindy, often accompanied by Dr. C. Peter Wagner and others are going to the nations teaching and activating thousands of ministers in "prophetic intercessory warfare prayer." They demonstrate to the national leaders how to discern the "strongman" over the nation and then destroy that ruling evil principality. This ministry helps that nation to become a sheep nation. It also causes the hearts of the leaders to turn to the people and the hearts of the people to turn to their leaders. Cindy, ministering with her powerful prophetic-apostolic anointing, has demonstrated that this works for regions, cities, national ministries and local churches.

Mass evangelism with the supernatural works of God has been reactivated by such men of God as Benny Hinn and Reinhard Bonnke. They are two of the best known international ministers who have tens of thousands attending their evangelistic campaigns. Many national evangelists are doing the same things in their countries. They are preparing the way for the apostles to arise in every nation to establish the converts on a firm foundation and build them into a mighty Church for Jesus Christ.

A New Apostolic Reformation?

The National Symposium on the Post-Denominational Church convened by Dr. C. Peter Wagner at Fuller Seminary, May 21-23, 1996 was a historical occasion in God's annals of Church history. It was prophetically orchestrated by the Holy Spirit to fulfill God's progressive purpose of bringing His Church to its ultimate destiny. Numerous denominational representatives were present with many delegates from other nations. The consensus of the panelists was that there are still apostles and prophets in the Church, and there is an emerging Apostolic Movement that will revolutionize the 21st-century Church. The last generation Church will have an Apostolic Reformation that will be as great as the first generation Apostolic Movement. The first generation Church prophets and apostles laid the foundation of the Church. Now the last day Apostolic Reformation will put the final finishing touches on the Church.

It will also bring revolutionary changes like the Protestant Movement brought forth in its day. The Protestant Movement started the era of the great reformation of the Church. The new Apostolic Movement will accelerate the final restorational work of the Holy Spirit causing it to be accomplished in one generation. The Great Reformation started the Church on its process of restoration of all truths, life experiences, and ministries that were in the early Church. God's purpose for the approximately 500 years of the reformation was ordained to bring the Church to a place of purity, ministry, and maturity as declared in Eph.4:13; 5:25,27.

The work of restoration will continue until members of Christ's corporate Body are taught, trained, activated, and matured in manifesting their membership ministries. There are multimillions of souls to be harvested for the purpose of incorporating them into the Body of Christ. God has predestined a certain quantity of members with Christlike qualities for the full functioning of His eternal Church. Jesus purchased, produced and is progressively perfecting His Church that He might present it to Himself as a glorious Church. His purpose is to use the Church to co-labor with Him in His eternal ministry (Eph.3:21; Rom.8:17).

Some of the Revolutionary Changes Perceived at This Point.

The new Apostolic Reformation will bring about the removal of many man made traditions within the Church. Such as the distinction between laity and clergy, spiritual and secular, members and ministers. There are Church members who are fulfilling their ministry as staff workers in a local church. There are those who are fulfilling their calling and ministry in the "secular" world. Regardless where members are functioning they are ministries in the Body of Christ. Church government and fivefold ministries are not to be deleted for there is structure and a chain of command in heaven as well as in the Church.

However, the position that is now called the "pastor" of a church will be redefined. Those who fill that position will function more like the coach of a sports team rather than the owner. The coach knows his calling is to teach, train, and equip each team member into their highest potential. He is to discover what team position each team member is best qualified to play. He develops the skills of each player while at the same time unifying them to play as one team. Their goal is not just to have fun but to enjoy fulfilling their part while playing to be winners over all the opposition.

The owner is more concerned about the team winning in order to bring in more paying participants. He is concerned about making payroll, making a profit, and building bigger stadiums. Too many of today's preachers function more like a team owner than a coach. Owners are interested in having a winning team to bring in great numbers of people for a bigger audience. The coach wants the numbers to come in so that he can have a greater team. The owner is in the numbers game of having a bigger audience to make him more successful. The coach is interested in equipping every player on his team to fulfill their greatest potential. The Apostolic Reformation will make church leaders and pastors more committed to raising up an army of equipped saints than an audience of paying spectators and fans.

Church cell home groups will increase and transition into doing the work of the ministry. The pastor will make sure everyone works together in fulfilling the pastor's vision for that local church. The senior headship for the local church (pastor) will no longer be a one man band but a band director. He will function as a choir director who makes sure all members not only sing their part well, but also be in harmony with all in the choir. The 21st-century Church will not function anything like the traditional church of today. Many leaders will not be able to make the transition because of their fear of losing control or lessening their authoritative position.

The Apostolic Reformation will cause believers to manifest the supernatural grace, gifts, and power of God. The one man show will be over. A few great demonstrators of God's power will become the multi-millions of demonstrators. The world will not exclaim "what a mighty man" but "what a mighty Church"! God will get all the glory through His Church not just through a few great ministers around the world.

Who Will Be the Leaders in the New Apostolic Reformation?

The leaders will be all fivefold ministers who have progressed from "called to be" to *chosen vessels* "being commissioned" to their ministry. They will be mature, seasoned men and women who have God's heart and mind for His Church. The ascension gift of the apostle will ? be fully restored during the Apostolic Reformation, but apostles will not be the only leaders. There will be apostolic and prophetic leaders who walk in present truth. They will have integrity and Christlike character with powerful supernatural ministries conducted in wisdom and maturity. There are those who have many revelations and prophecies confirming that they are "called to be an apostle" but they will not initially be the apostolic leaders. The apostolic fathers and leaders will be those whom God has commissioned to be apostles, prophets, evangelists, pastors, and teachers and are walking in all that the Prophetic and Apostolic Movements have restored.

APOSTOLIC has a broader meaning than just those called to be apostles. Apostolic will include all presently restored truth, miraculous ministries with signs, wonders, and miracles by ministers and church members. Apostolic fathers and leaders will be the ministers who have made the transition to the new divine order that God is establishing in His Church.

NETWORKING: There will be a new emphasis on prophetic and apostolic heads of denominations to network together. Networking does not imply that all groups should come under the headship of one great apostolic leader. Networking (a working net) is illustrated by a good fish net. Each network ministerial group or large church is like one of the knots that ties the lines together. Those who have vision, grace and wisdom to network with other networks will become the great fishing net that God will use to draw in the great multitude of souls.

The Post-Denominational Symposium or The New Apostolic Reformation Symposium has provided a place for all of these heads of networks, ministerial organizations and denominations to come together. This gives the Holy Spirit the opportunity to bring a greater unity and corporate vision within the Body of Christ.

The common meeting ground and corporate vision is reaping the great harvest and proclaiming Jesus as Lord over all the earth. The independent and denominational groups who believe the Apostles Creed, fundamentals of the Christian faith, and are walking in all restorational truth will be the ones with the greatest interest in networking. The religious Christian groups who are seclusive and exclusive, believing they are God's only true people will not be interested in networking with other Christian groups. Also those who are more interested in indoctrinating people in their religious "Christian" beliefs than in winning them to Jesus Christ will not be interested in networking. But there are many Christian groups who are interested in establishing God's kingdom more than their own. The Holy Spirit will draw those of like vision together to form a networking relationship to fulfill God's eternal purpose for the Body of Christ and planet earth.

The networking could be multi-level and world-wide. These same networks could be in each nation and continent on earth. There could be a national meeting of all these different networks from all levels of networking. There could also be an international meeting of all these heads of networks for unifying our corporate vision.

Networking will promote unity in the Body of Christ by connecting groups through intermediaries. Where two groups could not walk together a third may step into the gap and form a buffered link between them.

Every God-ordained network within the Body of Christ will have its part to play in fulfilling the overall vision of Jesus Christ, the Head of the Body. Some networks would have more of a hand ministry, others the eye, some the ear, feet, heart, and etc. Each major member (network) of the Body would have its own contribution to make for the functioning of the whole. Those who know what part of the Body they are and what their part in fulfilling the vision of the Head, will not be competitive, jealous, envious or critical of the others. For in the body the eye cannot say to the ear, or the mouth or to the hand - I have no need of you. We need each other. One network or denomination can never be the whole Body of Christ. We are all members of the **one universal many-membered corporate Body of Christ** under **one sovereign headship of Jesus Christ our Lord.** We all have only one Church to fulfill and one Kingdom to build and that is Christ's Church and God's Kingdom.

We see a model for this networking of networks in technology. The Internet is being heralded as a revolutionary tool for the world. It came into being by networking, that is, providing communication links, between existing networks. These networks represent various sectors of society, such as, government, military, education, science, banking, manufacturing, etc. The same synergistic explosion of progress seen in the Internet can be experienced by the corporate Church as denominations, ministries, networks, camps, fellowships, etc. begin to link together.

Preparation for God's Progressive Purposes. The Charismatic Renewal was the outpouring of the Holy Spirit upon all denominations. It made them realize that there was more than historic and fundamental church life. It broke up their fallow ground and activated them into supernatural experiences such as speaking in tongues. They experienced God's presence in praise. It renewed their first love and gave a desire for more of God. The present revival being called - "laughter, times of refreshing, floor time," and etc., is a preparatory move of the Holy Spirit the same as was the Charismatic

Renewal. The Charismatic Renewal was God preparing the Church for the Prophetic Movement. Now the present Refreshing Move of the Holy Spirit is preparing the Church for the great Apostolic Movement. Hundreds of ministers walking in present truth are already proclaiming and demonstrating that there are apostles in the Church today. The full restoration and demonstration of apostles are at hand.

The Timely Process for "GIDEON'S 300 Warrior Group" is Now Taking Place in the Church. We are now in the progressive stage where God is taking the Church to the refreshing river of testing and separation unto a greater responsibility of maturity and ministry. Hundreds of thousands have come and will continue to come to the present river of refreshing and blessing. Those who have been saturated with His presence will be challenged and tested at the river. Drinking at the refreshing river is not an end in itself. It is like Gideon's "river" which was a place of testing ones personal commitment, motive and character. The challenge is to maintain the **personal blessing** while moving into **corporate building**. We retain what we have while at the same time making the transition from **soaking** to **sending**, from **floor time** to **flowing time**, from just **soaking up His presence on the floor** to **taking up our warriors' weapons**.

From the 32,000 who came to Gideon's refreshing-revival less than one third continued on to the river of testing. Out of the 10,000 who drank at the river only three percent passed the test to become soldiers in Gideon's army. Less than one percent of the original participants made the transition and moved on to become part of God's chosen 300 mighty warriors.

From the thousands who are participating in the present Refreshing Move of the Holy Spirit only a small percentage will make the transition to become God's end time prophetic/apostolic warriors. Nevertheless, God will bring forth the "Gideon's 300" that He plans to use to put the enemy on the run. Jesus will choose those drinking at His river, who have the right spirit and attitude, to be a part of His "Gideon's Army." They are being prepared for the great end-time battle against the "Midianites" that are encamped against His Church.

A Personal Prophetic Vision of the Last Chapter of God's Book of His Mortal Church

The Lord Jesus gave me a vision while seeking Him with prayer and fasting. He showed me a great book. Its title was "The Book of the Mortal Church on Earth." He flipped through the Book until He came to a page titled, "The Last Chapter of the Mortal Church." He then turned a page at a time for me to see the page and paragraph headings. On some pages I was able to read most of the contents under the headings and on other pages only enough time was given to read the bold headings.

He said **some of His ministers** would only be shown one **page** or **paragraph** which would become their major message and ministry. They would have the anointing and responsibility to demonstrate and establish that part of the "Last Chapter" of His mortal Church.

He said He was showing me an **overview** and **highlights of the whole chapter** because He was giving me the responsibility to keep an overall perspective and make the progressive purpose of God known to His corporate Church. My personal ministry would major in the headings dealing with the full restoration of fivefold ministers and their ministry of equipping the saints. However, the panoramic picture and destiny for Christ's corporate Church would be my message and part to fulfill during the Last Chapter of the Mortal Church.

Following are some of the things I was allowed to see, especially those that the Holy Spirit is presently working with and implementing into the Church.

The Last Chapter Church - Divine Decrees and New Directives Being Made in Heaven.

New Assignments of the Angelic Host. More appearances of God's holy angels and the Devil's demonic manifestation are decreed to begin now and continue escalating until the coming of the Lord Jesus. There will be more and more discussions about angels and the spirit world on television talk shows until the world becomes obsessed with the idea of "other world" spirit beings.

God Has Released the Holy Spirit to Bring His Revelations and Activation to the End Time Church. This will bring forth the last generation of mortal **people**, unlimited **power**, new **products**, and more **places** dedicated to fulfilling God's present truth purposes.

Delay shall be no longer concerning the final preparation necessary for the kingdoms of this world to become the kingdoms of Christ Jesus and His Church. (Rev. 10:7; 11:15)

Activation of the second phase of apostles and prophets being fully restored to their rightful place of power and function. **Holy Spirit will intensify the maturing process for those who will be the participants.**

Jesus is maturing and motivating His fivefold ministers to intensify their training and equipping those who will be the soldiers in God's end-time army.

Local pastors must implement ministries that will reach the lost and establish and activate the saints while equipping them for their membership ministry in the Body of Christ.

Holy Spirit Has Been Commissioned to Accelerate His Restoration Work in the Church. A general overview of what accelerating restoration means: Restorational movements since AD1500 have accelerated in their frequency of occurrence from 300 years apart to 100 to 50 to every 10 years during the last half of the 20th century. Each prepared the way for the next over the past 500 years. The Protestant Movement prepared the way for the Holiness Movement and so on, the Pentecostal for the Latter Rain Restoration for the Charismatic Renewal and Faith Movement for the present Prophetic Movement which is now preparing the way for the Apostolic Movement which will in turn prepare the way for the Saints Movement enabling the saints of the Most High to fulfill Daniel 2:44; 7:18,22,27; Rev. 11:15; 1:5,6; 5:9,10.

Apostles and Prophets Arising in the World of Administration and Finances.

It is now time for activating the Joseph and Daniel company of apostles (Joseph) and prophets (Daniel) within the business field and political arena. The Esther and Deborah Company is arising right along with them. God is preparing an apostolic and prophetic company of Christian business people. They will not only bring the wealth of the wicked into the Church, but will affect the economy in many nations of the world. God is bringing the full transition of His "Joseph Company" from the status of prisoner to prime minister, and His "Daniel Company" from the lion's den to the right hand of the king.

The First Shall be Last and the Last Shall be First. What happened at the beginning of the Church will happen at the end of the Church Age. In fact, Scripture says "the glory of the latter house (last days Church) shall be greater than the former house (early Church). Jesus chose twelve men from the business world and ordained them as apostles. He did not choose men from the religious Rabbinical Schools or the Levitical Priesthood. Jesus made no distinction in calling and commissioning based on ones past professions or position in life. Revelation regarding God's thoughts concerning fivefold ministers is going to revolutionize the present thinking and function of the old church order. No scripture declares that a person must be the pastor of a church or have his own nonprofit organization to be called as an apostle or prophet in the Body of Christ. The U.S. government and religious leaders have designated who can be recognized as a minister within the church. God is raising up and giving recognition to His company of Joseph/Daniel-apostles/prophets. The old order Church system or the government may never recognize them for whom they are, but God is giving them His recognition and power to prosper. In the beginning of the Dark Ages of the Church religious men segregated God's people into **secular** and **spiritual**, **clergy** and **laity, business** and **church**. Everyone does not have to have a pulpit ministry to be a valid ministry in the Body of Christ. By the end of this century there will come revolutionary adjustments to the way God's Church functions on earth.

Apostles and Prophets to the Nations. Prophets and apostles will continue going to the nations of the world. They will be some of the main instruments God uses to reap the great end-time harvest. However, the primary anointing of the prophet is not manifested through mass evangelism or missions. That is the main mission and anointing of the evangelist. Prophets and apostles are divinely sent to give God's revelation and prophetic word for that nation. How that nation responds to God's Word will determine whether they become a goat or sheep nation. God will continue increasing His ministry of separating sheep nations from goat nations. (CI prophets have now gone to 40 nations, and in many of them God's prophetic word was spoken to the head of that nation. Many other prophets from other camps are doing the same things).

The Realignment of Nations. The shifting and realignment of nations as allies and enemies are taking place now. Secret meetings are now going on behind closed doors to bring these things to pass. China and some Islam nations are part of this process. The secret things will soon become public knowledge. Unless a tremendous revival happens within these nations, a great war between East and West will take place around the turn of this century. God will be progressively realigning the nations of the world in preparation for the final global conflict. The end result will be the exaltation of the righteous nations, while the wicked nations are subdued and come under the rule of the righteous.

Racial Strife and Rioting Reactivated! The Devil has plans to reactivate racial issues, not only black v.s. white, but other races and religions such as Jewish v.s. Christian. Islam and other cultic religions, occultic and humanist beliefs will try to make Christianity look like the problem and not the solution. They, of course, present themselves as the true group to resolve all the problems. The white supremacist and separatist group will continue to spark the flame that will start the fire roaring. Islamic radicals have plans to disrupt and hopefully overthrow and take over America by raising up a black militant Islamic following. Black and white Christians walking in present truth will become more unified while the anti-Christ religious system will propagate division, disunity, hatred, anger and rebellion. Prophetic intercessory prayer and warfare praise can stop, overturn and reverse the plans of the enemy. One international prophetess said that God revealed to her that if America as a nation does not turn to God like they should, then God was going to allow America to be ruled by Islam for a period of time. That would be worse than communism taking over.

Church Transitioning Toward Translation. A greater measure of revelation, faith and overcoming grace is being released in the Church. The mortal Church is in transition and preparation for becoming the immortal Church. The resurrection - translation of the saints which brings about the redemption of their mortal bodies into immortal, indestructible bodies will take place so that God can fulfill His greater purpose for and through His Church. There is a last day ministry designed for the overcoming Church to accomplish in the heavenlies and on earth which will require the saints to have their bodies redeemed. The redemption of the Body is the last act of redemption and **the last page of the last chapter of the mortal Church.** To be in the first phase of God's end time purpose will require complete death to self and full life in Christ Jesus. This includes dying to old religious traditions and living in all present truth. Submit to the death/life process that is being intensified in Christ's Church.

2

THE APOSTOLIC
MOVEMENT/REFORMATION

· · · · · · · · ·

A New Apostolic Movement is emerging
in this day and hour.   I have dealt with this
in detail in my new major book *"Apostles-
Prophets & The Coming Moves of God."* In this
booklet we want to enlighten you that there is
an Apostolic Reformation in process. It is
necessary for the fulfillment of all God's
purposes for His Church. The Apostolic
Movement is serving the same purpose as the
last five major movements called, The
Protestant, Holiness, Pentecostal, Charismatic
and The Prophetic Movement. Each of these
movements restored certain truths, ministries,
and spiritual experiences back into the
Church.

During the Dark Age of the Church all experiential truths and life-giving ministries were depleted. In one chapter of the new book we cover in abbreviated form what each of the movements restored including the ten major things that the Prophetic Movement restored back into the Church. The two major things that the Prophetic Movement restored were the ministry of the Prophet and a great company of prophets. The Apostolic Movement will do the same for the **apostle** as the Prophetic Movement did for the prophet.

God's Purpose for the Apostolic Movement.

Its main purpose is to cause the restoration of the Apostle, thus completing the full restoration of all fivefold ministers-- evangelist, pastor, teacher, prophet, apostle. Eph. 4:11-13. As the apostle is restored and all fivefold ministers are fulfilling the purpose for which God gave them to the Church, then it will launch the next restorational move of God. This will cause the greatest harvest of souls ever to take place on planet earth.

The Apostolic is destined to release the greatest manifestations of miracles, signs and wonders ever seen in one generation. God's righteous judgments will begin at the house of

God, the Church. It will then spread to the ungodly and the nations of the world. Reverential fear of God will be reestablished into the Church. Great persecution will come against the Church. The world economy will be shaken to the core. The true holy apostles and prophets of God will come to the forefront with Christ's answers for the Church and the world.

If the Church does not win the war in the heavenlies against Satan's plans, a Third World War will then be fought in the natural with the military forces of this world. If the nation of America does not show the fruit of repentance by turning from their wicked ways, and if the Church does not arise in intercessory prayer and warfare praise, and prevail against the plans of hell, then missiles will fall on major cities of America and strategic military areas. Millions will die throughout the nations of the world. All of this will be happening at the peak of the Prophetic-Apostolic movement.

However, the Apostolic Movement will launch the Church into its last three major restorational movements. The last three movements will fulfill all things, subdue all enemies and release Jesus to return and set up His kingdom over all the earth. (All the scriptural proof and examples of how this will transpire are covered in detail, in *"Apostles-Prophets and The Coming Moves of God."*)

What is the Apostolic Movement?

- It is a divine Restorational Move of God orchestrated by the Holy Spirit to bring Christ's Church to full maturity.

- It is ordained of God to bring the Church to the place where it fulfills God's divine destiny.

- It is destined to fulfill many scriptures by restoring more truth, spiritual experiences, and ministries of Christ back into the Church.

- It is the next step in God's restorational process.

- It is believing and accepting God's new revelation for His new breed of Apostles and Prophets.

What it is not!

- It is not reviving the Dark Age religious hierarchal order with a papal apostle headship.

- It is not a movement to exalt egotistical preachers to high positions of authority and dominion over others.

- It is not an end to itself, but a means to an end for the ultimate fulfillment of all things.

- It is not for exalting one fivefold minister over all the others.

- It is not exalting the Apostle and Prophet as the pinnacle and roof of the Church but to restore their servanthood position as the foundation of the Church. Jesus said that in His kingdom "the greatest of all is the servant of all." Mt. 23:11.

"APOSTLES-PROPHETS & THE COMING MOVES OF GOD"

· · · · · · · · ·

CHAPTER HEADINGS

- Why a Book about Apostles?
- What Is Happening Now?
- Biblical Perspectives of the Ministry of Apostles
- Apostles and Church Doctrine
- Apostles & Prophets and Fivefold Ministries
- Calling vs. Commissioning of Apostles or Prophets
- God's Desire and Purpose for Establishing His Church
- The Prophetic Movement and What it Restored
- The Special Ministries of Apostles and Prophets
- The Calling and Ministries of Fivefold Ministers
- Divine Progressive Preparation for the Apostolic Movement
- Extremes in the Restoration of Truth
- Apostolic Movement and its Potential Extremes
- The Last Day Ministry of Apostles and Prophets
- The Coming Moves of God
- The Saints Movement
- Army of the Lord And Eternal Judgment
- The Kingdom Establishing Movement
- Even So, Come, Lord Jesus!"

3

PROPHETIC
DESTINY

. . . .

In my 43 years of ministry I have found one of the most important truths to help a person maintain and mature in their ministry until they fulfill their prophesied destiny. Understanding the following reveals this truth: God's basis for calling a person to fulfill a divine destiny, to understand the divine process that God uses to take His children from their calling to their commissioning to fulfill their predestinated destiny.

For myself and many others the insights presented in this book have made the difference between success and failure. The criteria God uses for success is not the same as man's. According to God's standard a successful person is one who is progressively fulfilling the will of God toward their ultimate destiny in Christ Jesus. It is for those who are going through the four seasons of life whether spring, summer, fall, or winter. A peach tree in an orchard during winter with no leaves, blossoms, or fruit, with most of its life-giving sap down in its roots is just as much in the will of God as it is in the summer time with its abundance of peaches.

The major Bible Characters used to portray this truth reveal the divine process that God uses to enable those called to fulfill their prophetic destiny. When we understand God's principles and purposes for revealing a person's calling then we have a solid foundation for accepting and believing that calling. When we understand God's process for taking us from our calling to our commissioning it gives grace, patience, and wisdom to press on until we reach our ultimate fulfillment. All of us want to say with Apostle Paul "I have finished my course, run the race, and kept the faith." This truth will help us to be sure we hear Jesus say those all-important words, "well done good and faithful servant, enter thou into the eternal joy of the Lord." Mt.25:21,23; 2 Tim. 4:7.

"Behold the Goodness and the Severity of God" (Romans 11:22). This scripture reveals the nature of God and His dealings with His own Children. His goodness and mercy are shown in Him sovereignly calling us into His kingdom. It was God's love for the world and Christ's love and desire to have a Church/Bride, consisting of multimillions of members, that revealed the goodness of God. All of His members are to work together to fulfill Christ's overall purpose for His Church. The scriptures clearly teach that members of Christ's Church do not choose their membership ministry within the Body of Christ. Nor do ministers call themselves to a fivefold ministry of their own choosing. Jesus told the Twelve Apostles: "You have not chosen Me, but I have chosen you and ordained you" (John 15:16).

The gifts and callings of God are based on His sovereignty, not on human worthiness or persistence in requesting a position. Hours of prayer and weeks of fasting will show our desire and dedicated determination to be whatever God has called us to be and to become. But it will not buy a certain position in the Body of Christ or force

God to give us a ministry that He did not genetically design us to fulfill when He conceived and birthed us into His many-membered Church Body. The principle that Apostle Paul revealed when he said, "Behold the goodness and the severity of God," applies to all of God's children who have a membership ministry in His corporate Body. It also applies to His ascension gifts given to those who are to stand and minister in His office of apostle, prophet, evangelist, pastor, or teacher.

The goodness of God is manifested in the **gifts and callings He freely gives.** Our gifts of eternal life, the Holy Spirit and membership ministry are not based on who we are or what we have done but who God is and what He has done for us. His **severity** is revealed **in the process of His severe training** to make us ready to be commissioned to our divine **calling**.

To Whom Much is Given, Much is Required. Jesus has an incredible love for all members of His Church. But there seems to be a special love and dedication to those whom He has called to represent Him in His fivefold ministry. The Lord Jesus Christ has invested much of Himself into them: He has given them of His own nature, grace, gifts and ministry. And to whom much is given, much is required (Lk. 12:48). Those who are called to this realm of the ministry will go through a greater process of severe training before God commissions them to their fivefold office. They will also be judged by a much higher standard and more strictly than the regular members of the Body of Christ (James 3:1).

This principle seems to apply especially to those called to be **prophets** and **apostles.** Those apostles whom He has called to be special ambassadors for Him, and the prophets whom He calls to speak directly for God with a "Thus saith the Lord" are given a greater responsibility. Apostles and prophets have the dual ministry of laying the proper foundation for Christ's Church with the mutual divine enablement to receive supernatural revelation from God (Eph. 2:20; 3:5). But in the same way much more is required of them in obedience, integrity, righteousness and Christlikeness in all areas of their life. They are also required to minister more accurately and reveal God's specific word, will, and way more than any other ministries in the Body of Christ.

Essentials for Apostles and Prophets. There is a key scripture that all Body of Christ members must embrace into their attitude and actions if they are to make it through God's process from calling to commissioning. This has a special application to those with the high calling of apostle or prophet. They must never assume they have already attained their commissioning simply because they have received several supernatural confirmations of their calling and are ministering some in that calling. After many years of ministry, Apostle Paul made the following as a cry to God and a charge to the Church.

> *"But what things were gain to me, those I counted loss for Christ. Yea doubtless, and I count all things but loss for the excellency of the knowledge of Christ Jesus my Lord: for whom I have suffered the loss of all things and do count them but dung that I may win Christ, and be found in Him, not having mine own righteousness, which is of the law, but that which is through the faith of Christ, the righteousness which is of God by faith: That I may know Him, and the power of His resurrection, and the fellowship of His suffering, being made conformable*

unto His death; Not as though I had already attained, either were already perfect: but I follow after, if that I may apprehend that for which also I am apprehended of Christ Jesus. Brethren, I count not myself to have apprehended: but this one thing I do, forgetting those things which are behind, and reaching forth unto those things which are before, I press toward the mark for the prize of the high calling of God in Christ Jesus." (Phil. 3:8-14).

Paul declares that those who are going to make it from calling to commissioning must do these things. First, count everything as loss that would promote self-glory and self-preservation, not only count the loss, but suffer the loss. Second, never assume you have already attained to everything that God has called you to. Finally, forget all the successes and failures of the past, and then PRESS with all that is within you TOWARD THE MARK for the PRIZE of the HIGH CALLING of God you have in Christ Jesus.

Many are Called, But Few are Chosen. It is interesting to note the two occasions when Jesus made this statement in Matthew 20:16 and 22:14. One was in reference to a persons' attitude and the other was to a lack of proper preparation. The first was a wrong attitude in relating to how God rewards His laborers who work for different durations of time in His vineyard. The other statement was made at the end of His parable about the person who had received the calling to be an attendee at the king's wedding for his son, but did not make the proper preparation to fulfill that calling. I understand in this context that the word "chosen" is synonymous with the word "commissioned" and it would therefore be hermeneutically correct to make the following statement, "Many are called but few are commissioned." In other words, there are many in the Body of Christ who receive a high ministerial calling in Christ Jesus, but because of their attitude and lack of proper preparation never press all the way through to their commissioning to that high calling. Therefore, it would be the same to say, "Many are called but few ever reach their commissioning to their high calling in Christ Jesus." The winning overcomers are not those who start the race at their CALLING but those who finish the race to their COMMISSIONING and remain FAITHFUL to it until the end. "Those that are with Him are CALLED, and CHOSEN, and FAITHFUL (Rev. 17:14).

There are many examples of God's process of calling a person to the position of a prophet, apostle or king. In most cases there is a long period of apprenticeship, training, testing and trying before God commissions them to that calling. If there was greater understanding of this principle within the Body of Christ it would take much of the confusion out of those who are called, but are not fully fulfilling what they know they are called to be and do.

A person receives a divine call from God usually by revelation knowledge, vision, dream, a deep conviction or a personal prophecy from a prophet or prophetic presbytery. The general assumption is that if God sovereignly reveals what we are called to be, for example, an apostle, the tendency is to immediately start trying to fulfill our concept of an apostle. This always brings much confusion and frustration to the person trying to be what they are not yet prepared to be. It not only affects them but their mate, family and anybody they are working with. A person trying to fulfill a ministry before God's timing is like an engine trying to run smoothly with the timing gear completely out of proper timing.

We must always remember that God is

the one who gives a divine calling. He initiates it, not the person. Fivefold ministries, gifts of the Holy Spirit and ministries in the Church are not set out on God's "smorgasbord-table" for us to pick and choose as we will. "But now **God has set** the members in the Body just **as He pleased**," But one and the same Spirit works all these things, distributing to each one individually **as He wills**." "And **God has appointed** these in the Church: first apostles, second prophets . . ." But to each one of us **grace was given** according to the measure of **Christ's gift**," "And **He Himself gave** some to be apostles, some prophets . . ." (1Cor.12:11,18,28; Eph.4:7,11).

We cannot expect a positive response from God if we say, "I choose to be a pastor, I don't want to be a prophet or I want to be an apostle, not a teacher." God does the choosing and appointing. We do the responding with a yes or no, acceptance or rejection. However, if we reject, then God starts the process of making us willing to say yes. He will continue that for a period of time until He determines that we are not going to respond, at which time He transfers the calling and anointing to another vessel who is willing. There are examples in the Bible of this happening as it did with Saul and David, or Esau and Jacob. If the person gives a positive response then God directs the Holy Spirit to start the process of taking them from the state of "CALLED TO BE" to "COMMISSIONED TO BEING" an apostle and manifesting apostolic signs and wonders. The scriptures even declare that the angels are assigned to help those heirs of this great salvation and those who accept their calling to demonstrate their special portion of God's grace and glory. (Heb.1:14.)

Biblical Examples of God's Process for Taking a Person from Calling to Commissioning:

DAVID: The shepherd boy with a prophetic minstrel anointing but called to be king over all Israel. He is a good example of this process. Let us look at David's preparation between calling and commissioning.

He was called at approximately the age of 13. David was faithfully shepherding his father's sheep when he was summoned to appear before the prophet Samuel. God gave David his kingly ministry calling through the laying on of hands and prophecy. At that time,

Prophet Samuel anointed him with holy oil to be king and the Spirit of God came on him with a kingly anointing. Nevertheless, that did not put David in the position or ministry of being a king. It did not make his brethren recognize him as a king. David did not make his name cards with the title "King David" and a statement on it declaring, "I have been prophesied a kingship calling and have been anointed to be a king, call me if you need the ministry of a king." I have seen some young ministers who received a prophecy that they were called to be prophets. They immediately made name cards "Prophet So-and-So" with a statement on it saying, "I have been called and anointed to be a prophet. Call me if you need the ministry of a prophet."

Called to be an Apostle? What does one do when the revelation comes that one is called to be an apostle? That person should say to God, "Lord, I accept the calling of an apostle. Now I give you my full permission for you to start the intensified process of training me from 'called to be' to Your commissioning for me to BE the apostle you want me to be." That is the first thing anyone can do at that stage of their life and ministry.

It would not be wise to immediately start

doing certain things. First, do not get the 'Moses Syndrome' and begin arguing and debating with God. Do not make statements that imply God didn't really evaluate you before He revealed such a calling. Do not start making excuses about why you cannot be and do what He has prophesied to you. Do not try to explain to the all-knowing and all-powerful God why it couldn't happen. Do not make such insulting remarks to God. God does not call the qualified but qualifies the called. The Bible reveals that those who argue and debate with God at their calling rarely ever fulfilled their ultimate destiny.

During the last few years, I have seen some young pastors of small churches receive prophecies that they are called to be apostles. Some immediately changed their name cards from "Rev" or "Pastor" to "Apostle" and began trying to plant churches and solicit other ministers whom they can father. Some want to begin writing their book on the ministry of the apostle, right away. Usually these called ones are very sincere and are doing what they think they are supposed to do. But most times the called one has a lack of proper understanding. They have more presumption than faith, more zeal than wisdom, more revelation than reality, and more gifted ministry than manhood maturity. This type of person usually makes the wrong response and causes an improper representation of the divine ministry of an apostle.

So What is the Process and Why Does God Choose to Do It This Way? One reason is that God must make the man before He can release the ministry. The Christlike character of the person called to a ministry is the foundation for the quality, quantity and lasting ability of the ultimate ministry of the called one. For instance, if a person lays a two foot foundation for a three story house, then that is all he can build. If he takes a longer time, uses more material and effort to go down two or three stories underground in laying his foundation then he can build a 30 to 50 story building. If he wants to build a one hundred story building then much more preparation is required. In other words, provision is based on preparation. The height of the building is based on the quality of the foundation. If a 50 story building was suddenly placed on a five-story building foundation, it would crush it and the building would crumble to the ground.

As an example, when I was a 20 year old pastor, I prayed, fasted and begged God to give me a powerful ministry and anointing that would affect the whole church world. Without knowing it I was asking God to do for me then what He is doing now. However, if God had dropped on me back then this "multi-story building" ministry that I have now it would have crushed me. My foundation of preparation, experience and maturity of manhood and ministry was just a basic one- story foundation at that time. Over the last 43 years of ministry there have been four major times when God has torn down my manhood and ministry building, ripped out my limited foundation, dug deep down into my earth removing it and pouring in His cement while replacing my old structure with His greater steel beams. I am convinced that God has given the Holy Spirit the same prophetic ministry that He gave to Prophet Jeremiah. ". . .To root out and to pull down, To destroy and to throw down, To build and to plant." (Jer.1:10). Notice, there are twice as many words devoted to the preparative process as there are to the building and planting. The greater and more in-depth the preparation the greater the man and the mightier the ministry can be. It is the law of cause and effect, preparation and provision, calling and commissioning at work.

The books of First and Second Samuel record the life of David from his calling to be king of Israel to his inauguration as king over all Israel and his following 40 years of kingship ministry. He was 'called to be' at age thirteen but it was seventeen years later before he had a partial fulfillment of that prophecy. He was made king over the tribe of Judah when he was 30 years old, but it was more than seven years later before he became king over all Israel. He had a 24-year process of going from 'called to be a king' to 'being a king'. Most of the Psalms are prayers that David prayed while he was going through stages of ministry and God's preparative process. Let's now look at the different processes David had to go through and the ministries that he had to be faithful in before God fulfilled his personal prophecy of being a king.

1. David was faithful in shepherding his father's sheep before and after his anointed calling.
2. He was faithful in his bear and lion killing ministry of protecting his

father's sheep.

3. He willingly ministered to the needs of his brothers who were already in their soldiering ministry.

4. He boldly fulfilled his giant killing ministry. (He didn't get exalted with people's praises).

5. He was faithful in his music ministry to king Saul. (He didn't say, "I am sorry but I wasn't called to sing for the king, I was called to be a king!")

6. He was faithful in his position when Saul made him captain of a thousand soldiers. David had an appreciative and humble attitude. He did not say, "my prophecy from Prophet Samuel said nothing about being a lowly captain, I'm called to the position of king."

7. He stayed true to God during his time of having to run and hide from the persecution of Saul. He could have developed a spirit of rejection, a persecution complex, a sense of abandonment and bitterness against leadership. The records in First and Second Samuel and the Psalms reveal the attitude David took that kept this from happening. It is not just what one

goes through that causes the inner problems that need inner healing much later but the attitude we take and our response toward them.

8. He was faithful and true to God while giving his best service to the heathen headship he was under when he had to go outside of Israel and live in the land of the Philistines for a period of time. David went from his closest possibility for his prophecy being fulfilled to the furthest and most remote possibility of it ever being fulfilled. The old saying, "It is the darkest just before the dawn" is very applicable to a person who is about to come into their ultimate calling and prophesied destiny. This is exemplified in the life of Joseph, David, Jesus and in Moses seeking to fulfill his prophetic word concerning bringing Israel out of Egypt.

9. He did not give up during his darkest hour when all of his wives and children and those of his 600 men were captured and all their possessions taken from his headquarters at Ziklag. For the first time in his life his own men were turning against him and blaming him for their grief and loss. But David

"encouraged himself in the Lord", rallied his men together, pursued the enemy and recovered all and equally distributed it among his men. Those who stayed behind guarding the stuff received the same portion as those who went to the battle. He manifested fairness, equity, unselfishness, courage and faith to pursue, attack and take back all that was his plus all the possessions of those who had stolen from him. Those who give in to discouragement during their "darkest hour before the dawn of prophetic fulfillment" will miss their day of opportunity and not fulfill their ultimate ministry.

10. While David was going through his lowest ebb and greatest test of his life, the person who was occupying his prophesied position was killed in battle. After the position of king was vacated because of the death of Saul on the battlefield, the elders of Judah called David to come and be king over the tribe of Judah. This was David's heritage, for he was a descendant of Judah. When we maintain our

integrity and faith during our greatest trial, God makes a way for us to take dominion over our heritage.

The other tribes put one of Saul's sons as king over them. The position that rightly belonged to David was temporarily given to someone who had no divine right to it. God had already declared through Prophet Samuel that Saul's posterity had been cut off from ruling over Israel. God had already canceled Saul's continued kingship over Israel because he had not taken seriously the prophet's personal prophecies to him and had failed on two occasions to do everything the prophecies told him to do, (1 Sam. 13:13,14; 15:28,29; 16:1.)

Though David knew that he rightfully belonged in the position as king over all Israel, he did not demand his own rights or try to make the elders vote him in as king over all the tribes. He waited more than seven years for God's timing and providential workings for all the tribes to request him to take his place as king over all Israel. He did not take advantage of his opportunity to remove king Saul by killing him while being persecuted in the wilderness. He even blessed the seed of Saul who had forced him to remain in a wilderness area and seemingly been a hindrance to David seeing the fulfillment of his prophecies for many years. There are many check points and tests during the process from people's prophetic calling to commissioning to their ordained major ministry. How one responds and adjusts to these processes of God will determine the degree of prophetic fulfillment.

11. Finally, after 24 years of God's progressive preparative process David realizes the complete fulfillment of his personal prophecy concerning being king over all Israel. What a joyful sense of destiny and fulfillment it brings when God's prophesied purpose actually comes to pass. David was finally commissioned to the office of king according to God's full purpose. It launched him into 40 years of successful ministry as king over all Israel. Do not settle for partial fulfillment of God's prophetic destiny

for your life. Be patient, enduring and persevering until you receive and fulfill all that God has prophetically promised. Be not weary in well doing for you will reap in God's due season if you faint not. Therefore do not cast away your confidence, which has great reward. For you have need of endurance, so that after you have done the will of God, you may receive your prophetic promise. (Gal.6:9; Heb.10:35,36)

There are several more biblical examples which we will only use as condensed specific illustrations of this truth concerning the lengthy period of time between calling and commissioning. A divinely called one cannot bypass God's process. You can pray, prophesy, decree and confess your way through, but there is nothing you can do to exempt yourself from it. Paul and Peter declare that this fiery process must try every person's works and attitudes. Everything that is wood, hay or stubble shall be burnt up but that which is gold and silver will be brought to a higher grade of purity. For the trying of your faith is more precious than gold to God. Therefore, think it not strange concerning the fiery process which shall try all of us, but rejoice knowing that tribulation develops patience and produces that which makes us not ashamed to believe, endure and press on until we receive our ultimate ministry and fulfill our ultimate destiny. (1 Cor 3:13; 1 Pet 1:8).

ELISHA: Called to be a Prophet to Israel. He had to spend a twelve-year apprenticeship from his calling to his commissioning. After Elijah came out of his cave of despair, God spoke to him to anoint Haziel to be king over Syria, Jehu to be king over Israel. "And Elisha the son of Shaphat of Abel Meholah you shall anoint as prophet in your place." 1 Kings 19:16-21. He found Elisha plowing in the field with twelve yokes of oxen. Elijah came to him and threw his mantle upon Elisha. He knew from this act that he had just been called to be Elijah's apprentice to inherit his prophetic anointing. He sacrificed two of his oxen as an offering unto the Lord and had a feast for his people, kissed his father and mother good bye. "Then he arose and followed Elijah, and became his servant." Notice the prophetic call made a wealthy farmer be willing to forsake all of his wealth and prestige to become the servant of a major prophet. This reveals some of the qualities that he would need to press on to receive the double-portion-anointing of his mentor.

For twelve years Elisha served Elijah by carrying his luggage, preparing his meals and all the other things that a servant would do for his master. There are no records that Elisha ever performed any miracles or prophesied to anyone during those 12 years. Finally the test came to see whether Elisha would make it over the last hurdle. The story unfolds in Second Kings chapter two. Four times Elisha had the opportunity to miss out on his commissioning to be the prophet who would take Prophet Elijah's place as God's voice to Israel.

Elijah knew where the Lord wanted him to be when he was to be taken to heaven in a whirlwind and God's fiery chariots. He knew that Elisha had to be there to see him ascend to heaven in order to receive his prophetic mantle. Knowing this, Elijah gave Elisha his final exams before graduating him to his position. They stopped at Gilgal, Bethel, Jericho and the Jordan River. At each place Elijah told Elisha "Stay here, please, for the Lord has sent me on to . . ." but each time Elisha responds with settled determination in his voice, "As the Lord lives, and as your soul lives, I will not leave you!" God always checks us out to see how committed we are to going all the way with Him to receive everything that has been prophetically promised. He had invested 12 years to come to this place and he was not about to allow anything to cause him to come short of God's ultimate for his life and ministry.

Not only did his master try to talk him into staying but his prophetic brethren tried to discourage him. Prophets came out of their school of prophets at Bethel and Jericho and before they crossed over Jordan saying to Elisha "Don't you know that your master is going to be taken away from you today? Why do you continue to stick with him when he is going to be gone before the day is over?" Each time Elisha emphatically replied with determined finality, "Yes, I know; keep silent!" At the Jordan river Elijah took his mantle and struck the water and it parted, and the pathway across Jordan dried up immediately and they crossed over on dry ground.

Make it to God's Appointed Place and Time. Elisha Made It! Then the revelation was given to reveal why it was necessary for Elisha to have stuck with him like a leach. "And so it was, when they had crossed over, that Elijah said to Elisha, 'Ask! What may I do for you, before I am taken away from you?' Elisha said, 'Please let a double portion of your spirit be upon me.' So he said, 'You have asked a hard thing. Nevertheless, **if you see me when I am taken from you, it shall be so for you; but if not, it shall not be so.**" (2 Kings 2:9,10). In other words if Elisha had stayed anywhere along the way and had not been there to see Elijah taken up to heaven he would not have received the mantle of Elijah and his commissioning to be the major prophet to Israel as Elijah had been. His twelve year apprenticeship would have counted for nothing if he had not determinedly pressed on through that final day. He could have discouraged himself by thinking "Elijah has not shared any of his anointing with me for these twelve years. I don't think he is going to follow through and let me have his mantle." I have seen many who had faithfully served a ministry for years hoping to inherit a leadership role or the mighty ministry of the man of God, but they became impatient, lost faith in the leadership and forsook the ministry and the man of God just before they would have received everything. Once you have been called and placed in a position of apprenticeship, stay with dedicated determination and stick-to-it-ness until you have received what you originally set out to receive.

Oh the Joy and Reward of Ultimate Fulfillment. Elisha had stuck in there until he saw Elijah ascend to heaven. As he ascended up he threw his mantle back to Elisha. He wanted to check it out to see if he had finally received what he had believed for all these years. He had just seen Elijah part the Jordan by striking it with the mantle he now held in his hands. "Then he took the mantle of Elijah that had fallen from him, and struck the water, and said, 'Where is the Lord God of Elijah?' And when he also had struck the water, it was divided this way and that; and Elisha crossed over. Now when the sons of the prophets who were from Jericho saw him, they said, 'The spirit of Elijah rests on Elisha.' And they came to meet him, and bowed to the ground before him." Those who had ridiculed him just a few hours before now acknowledged that Elisha had inherited Prophet Elijah's powerful anointing as God's major prophet to Israel. The records of the two prophets show that Elisha truly did receive the double portion for he performed twice as many miracles in his ministry as Elijah. After pressing through his darkest hour and greatest test, Elisha received the double portion anointing and was launched into more than 50 years of successful ministry. There is no joy and sense of accomplishment like that of finally receiving what you have been believing and pursuing for many years.

JOSEPH: Called to be a Ruler and a Savior. His life dramatically reveals the process God may take some through between their calling and commissioning to their supernaturally revealed destiny. Joseph received his calling through two prophetic dreams when he was 17 years old. (Gen.37:2-11). But it was 13 years before he saw a partial fulfillment of his calling and another two years before he saw his dreams come to pass exactly as he had seen it. From the moment he received his dreams and revealed them to his brethren and father things began to fall apart around him. He went from being his father's favored son with a royal robe to having that robe ripped off by his jealous brothers. They stripped him and threw him into a pit with the intent of letting him die there. But some Ishmaelite merchantmen came along and so his brothers sold Joseph to them for twenty pieces of silver. The Ishmaelites took him to Egypt and sold him to Potiphar, an Egyptian captain of the guards over all the prisons in Egypt.

Negative Circumstances vs. God's Presence and Will. It is good to know that our circumstances do not determine whether God is with us and directing the affairs of our lives. Thank God, the Bible declares that "The LORD was with Joseph, and he was a successful man; and he was in the house of his master the Egyptian. And his master saw that the LORD was with him and that the LORD made all he did to prosper in his hand. So Joseph found favor in his sight, and served him. Then he made him the overseer of his house, and all that he had he put under his authority. So it was, from the time that he had made him the overseer of his house, and all that he had, that the LORD blessed the Egyptian's house for Joseph's sake; and **the blessing of the LORD was on all that he had in the house and in the field. Thus he left all that he had in Joseph's hand, and he did not know what he had except for the bread which he ate. Now Joseph was handsome in form and appearance.**" (Genesis 39:2-6). These scriptures reveal some of the attitudes and activities that Joseph experienced during his humbling and depressing process. He worked hard for his heathen master with a willing spirit and joyful attitude. Because of Joseph's calling, attitude and anointing God blessed all that he did for Potiphar. God promoted him to be the overseer of all of Potiphar's business and household. This gave him a ray of hope that he might be progressing to the position where his prophetic dreams could be fulfilled.

Setbacks and Unjust Treatment vs. God's Process and Purposes. Suddenly all of Joseph's hopes and possibilities were dashed to pieces. Because Joseph was such a handsome and charming man, Potiphar's wife began to lust after him. She demanded that he commit adultery with her. Joseph exemplified a virtuous character. He declared to her that he could not do this for it would betray loyalty to his master and the trust that Potiphar had put in him. But most of all it would cause him to sin against his God. Nevertheless, she persisted day after day until the opportunity arose when there was no one in the house but the two of them. She grabbed him by his tunic and tried to force him to bed with her. He pulled away but she held on. He got away but his tunic was left in her hands. **A person scorned and rejected becomes a bitter enemy.** She falsely accused

Joseph of trying to rape her showing her husband the tunic as proof. The husband believed her and became so angry with Joseph that he had him thrown into the prison where the king's prisoners were confined. Can God be allowing such things to happen to His chosen ones? Joseph was innocent and righteous in all his doings, but he was still unjustly treated, convicted and sentenced as though he was completely guilty. Why didn't God protect him and defend his righteous integrity? Could all of these negative experiences be providential in bringing Joseph to the place where his prophetic dreams would come to pass? Yes, for in this prison he made the contacts and had the experience which resulted in him being in position for commissioning to his ordained ministry. Righteous acts are not always immediately rewarded. But they keep us in good standing with God so that He can progressively move us on to our ultimate ministry. He was unjustly thrown into jail but the scriptures declare, "And he was there in the prison. But the LORD was with Joseph and showed him mercy, and He gave him favor in the sight of the keeper of the prison. And the keeper of the prison committed to Joseph's hand all the prisoners who were in the prison; whatever they did there, it was his doing. The keeper of the prison did not look into anything that was under Joseph's authority, because the LORD was with him; and whatever he did, the LORD made it prosper." (Gen.39:20-23).

When Setbacks and Demotions are Setups for Promotion. What we need to know more than anything else is "If the Lord is with us?". Not our apparent successes or failures nor our circumstances, but whether the Lord Jesus is **WITH US**. After about two years in this prison God caused the king's butler and baker, who had been committed to the same prison, to each have a dream. Joseph's interpretation of these dreams was that the butler would be restored to his ministry with the king but the baker would be killed. He asked the butler to bring his name before the Pharaoh in hopes that he would release him from prison. But two more years passed by, for a total of four years, before the butler remembered him.

Pharaoh had a very disturbing dream that his psychics, astrologers, magicians and wise men could not interpret. The butler suddenly remembered Joseph and mentioned how he had interpreted their dreams and they had come to pass just as he had described their meanings. The Pharaoh summoned Joseph who then interpreted his dream as predicting seven years of plentiful crops and then seven years of famine. He then proceeded to give Pharaoh the wisdom as to what to do. He should select a discerning and wise man to set as lord over all the land of Egypt. "And the advice was good in the eyes of Pharaoh and in the eyes of all his servants. And Pharaoh said to his servants. 'Can we find such a one as this, a man in whom is the Spirit of God?' Then Pharaoh said to Joseph, 'Inasmuch as God has shown you all this, there is no one as discerning and wise as you. You shall be over my house and all my people shall be ruled according to your word; only in regard to the throne will I be greater than you.' Then Pharaoh took his signet ring off his hand and put it on Joseph's hand; and he clothed him in garments of fine linen and put a gold chain around his neck. And he had him ride in the second chariot which he had; and they cried out before him, 'Bow the knee!' So he set him over all the land of Egypt. And Pharaoh called Joseph's name Zaphnath-Paaneah. And he gave him as a wife Asenath, the daughter of Poti-Pherah Priest of On. So Joseph went out over all the land of Egypt. Joseph was thirty years old when he stood before Pharaoh king of Egypt." (Gen.41:37-44).

Prisoner to Prime Minister in One Day. Thus, after thirteen long years Joseph has progressed from "called to be" to "being," from calling to commissioning, from prisoner to prime minister. When Pharaoh put his signet ring and new clothing of fine linen on him, Joseph was launched into the full time ministry that he had been called to fulfill. We see how important it is for one to keep the right attitude, resist temptation, retain integrity and never stop giving one's best in every unjust and humbling situation that seems to be a setback to the progress toward one's ultimate objective. God rewards faithfulness. Joseph's trouble started when he began his ministry of dreams and interpretations. But it was dreams and interpretation of dreams that made the way for him to be launched into his ministry. Never say, "I am never going to do this or that ministry again because it was what caused my brothers to turn against me and gave me thirteen years of horrible experiences." If so you will miss the very thing that God had arranged for your deliverance.

Prophetic Dreams are Finally Fulfilled.
Nine years later his brothers came to buy corn
and fulfilled the first dream by bowing before
him. Then Jacob and all his 66 descendants
came and bowed before Joseph which fulfilled
his second dream. Joseph gave full forgiveness
and restoration to his brothers who had so
wronged him. He brought them to Egypt to
be a part of his ministry and blessed them
with the area of Goshen, the best pasture land
in Egypt. After Jacob died at the age of 147
his brothers came and begged Joseph not to
take vengeance on them. Because of the
revelation he had received about all that had
transpired he was able to say with heartfelt
conviction, "Do not be afraid, for am I in the
place of God? But as for you, **you meant evil
against me**; but **God meant it for good**, in
order to **bring it about** as it is this day, to
save many people alive." Joseph received the
same revelation that Apostle Paul shared with
the Roman Christians. "And **we know that
all things work together for good** to those
who **love God**, to those who are the **called
according to His purpose**." This is a vital
understanding and attitude for a person to
have in order to make it through the process.
Because Joseph maintained the proper

attitude and took correct actions during his testing and trying process he was commissioned to his exalted position of being the savior not only of his headquarters area in Egypt but of his own kindred. He went from prisoner to prime minister in one day. At the age of 17 he was called but at the age of 30 he was commissioned and launched into 80 years of successful ministry concluding it at the age of 110 when he died.

ABRAHAM: Called to be Father of Many Nations. His life also portrays this truth. Since I am in the process of writing a book on "Prophet Abraham, The Father of us All," I will not give the details of his life. He was called at the age of around 50 to be the father of many nations. He was to leave all of his kindred and go stake out a land that God would give to his heritage. His first attempt at fulfilling this word fell short of the promised land. He took all his family and traveled to Haran in Mesopotamia which was 200 miles beyond Canaan. He stayed there for 25 years until his father died. He was 75 years old when he launched out again to fulfill his prophetic calling. This time he overshot the land of Canaan by around 200 miles ending up in Egypt. He finally came back from Egypt and stopped in the middle of the land of Canaan. The Lord speaks to him that this is the land.

Trying to help God fulfill prophecy produces an 'Ishmael' ministry or business. They decided to help God fulfill their prophecy after ten years in the land and not being able to produce a child. Trying to fulfill a calling with human reason and logic caused them to produce a child, Ishmael, which was not God's choice. Ishmael represents a ministry that is born of the flesh, brought into existence by man's manipulation and not by the Spirit and will of God. Then fourteen years later God told Abraham that he had missed it. Ishmael was not the son that God had promised him. God changed Abraham's status from "called to be" to "being" the father of many nations. After 50 years [Abraham 100, Sarah 89], Abraham had progressed from his calling to God commissioning him by enabling Sarah to conceive and bring forth the promised son.

God's Progressive Prophecies and Testing Process. During his life Abraham received **eleven personal prophecies** and went through **seven major tests.** When he passed each test, God increased his prophetic promises. The last major test took place twenty five years after Isaac was born. God asked him to take Isaac, his only son, whom he deeply loved and offer him as a burnt offering upon an altar. He took the wood and fire. He laid the wood on the altar and then tied Isaac on top of it. He took his knife and was ready to stab it into Isaac's heart, when suddenly the angel of the LORD shouted for Abraham to stop! "And He said, 'Do not lay your hand on the lad, or do anything to him; for now I know that you fear God, since you have not withheld your son, your only son, from Me" (Gen.22:12).

There is a Place Beyond Calling and Commissioning. When God saw the unquestioning obedience of Abraham to take what all his prophetic promises were wrapped in and destroy it, God changed His word to him from a conditional personal prophecy to a ratified oath. God swore on His honor and eternal name that nothing could keep all that He had promised Abraham from coming to pass. "By Myself I have sworn, says the LORD, **because you have done this thing**, and have not withheld your son, your only son-- 'blessing I will bless you, and multiplying I will multiply your descendants as the stars of the heaven and as the sand which is on the seashore; and your descendants shall possess the gate of their enemies. In your seed all the nations of the earth shall be blessed, **because you have obeyed My voice**.' So Abraham returned to his young men, and they rose and went together to Beersheba; and Abraham dwelt at Beersheba." (Gen.22:16-19)

Obedience and Patience Appropriates. Thus, we find that it took a fifty-year process for Abraham to go from "called to be a father" to "being a father." It took another twenty five years for God to take Abraham to the ultimate test that would bring him into a relationship and covenant with God that very few of God's people ever reach. As in natural schooling, the teacher cannot pass students on to the next grade level until they pass the test. The scripture in Gen.22:1 says, "God **tested** Abraham." We should understand the positive purposes of God's tests and not fear or resist them, for they are God's way of determining if we are ready for promotion. It is amazing that the eternal God who knows all things said to Abraham, after he had demonstrated that he would do anything God asked, "**now I know that you fear God**." Many are called but few are chosen or commissioned. How we respond to God's preparative process of trying and testing determines if we will ever reach the status of being chosen and commissioned. Whether or not we pass the ultimate test determines whether our descendants will carry on our ministry. If we pass the ultimate test then God will change our conditional prophecies to unconditional prophetic decrees which are backed by God's own sworn oath. He will personally make sure that every prophetic promise comes to pass.

JESUS CHRIST: Called to be Redeemer, Head of the Church and King of the Universe. The prophets of old prophesied His ministry according to God the Father's will and purpose for Him. In the fullness of time He was supernaturally conceived in the womb of Mary and then birthed into this world. He was the perfect and holy Son of God who lived a sinless life. He was called from His birth but it was thirty years later before God commissioned Him to do the work which He had come to do on earth. He had thirty years of God's preparative process but only three and one-half years of ministry. Jesus spent thirty years of His life in God's preparatory process and only three and one-half years in His ministry. That is a ratio of about ten to one. If the Father felt that Jesus, the sinless Son of God, needed this much preparation before He could be commissioned to His preordained ministry, then how much more do you and I need to go through God's preparation process. Jesus had to go through the major test of fasting 40 days and nights and then being tempted with the Devil's greatest strategies and manipulating powers. After He passed this test, "God anointed Jesus of Nazareth with the Holy Spirit and with power, who went about doing good and healing all who were oppressed by the Devil, for God was **with** Him." Acts 10:38. When Jesus was baptized in water, Father God said "this is My beloved Son in whom I am well pleased." But it was when Jesus passed the test in the wilderness that God commissioned Him to begin His miraculous ministry.

After Jesus fulfilled three and one-half years of ministry God put Him to His ultimate test to see if He could be promoted to be head over all things to His universal Church. When He went through the Garden of Gethsemane He suffered incomprehensibly in His soul and will. He cried out in heartbreaking anguish, Father, if it be possible let this cup of suffering pass from Me, nevertheless, not My will but Thine be done. He endured incredible physical suffering from the beatings, the crown of thorns, 39 lashes on His back and finally the most excruciating pain of being crucified on a wooden cross and hanging there until His body expired in physical death. He paid the highest price of personally suffering even unto death. Because He was willing and obedient to pay the extreme price He was exalted to the highest position heaven had to offer. "Jesus made Himself of no reputation, taking the form of a bond-servant, and coming in the likeness of men. And being found in appearance as a man, He humbled Himself and became obedient to the point of death, even the death of the cross. Therefore God also has highly exalted Him and given Him the name which is above every name, that at the name of Jesus every knee should bow, of those in heaven, and of those on earth, and of those under the earth, and that every tongue should confess that Jesus Christ is Lord, to the glory of God the Father." (Phil.2:7-11).

The attainment of Jesus' ultimate position was dependent upon His willingness to go through the ultimate testing process of suffering and death. He learned obedience and full submission to God through the things which He suffered while in His mortal body. Those who fulfill their ultimate destiny will have gone through all three phases of the overcomer. "They overcame him (the Devil who is the accuser of the saints) by the blood of the Lamb and by the word of their testimony, and **they did not love their lives to the death.**" (Rev.12:11) The only ones who will be exalted to the high position of ruling and reigning with Christ will be those who are willing to suffer the complete death of the self-life, being fully crucified with Christ, and not trying to preserve our lives but laying down our lives at the foot of the cross of Jesus. Becoming children of God by being washed in His blood and born of His Spirit does not guarantee full heirship with Christ Jesus. "If children then heirs--heirs of God and joint heirs with Christ, **if indeed we suffer with Him**, that we may also be glorified together. For I consider that the **sufferings** of this present time are not worthy to be compared with the glory which shall be revealed in us." To him that **overcomes** I will grant to sit with Me on My throne, as I also overcame and sat down with My Father on His throne." He that overcomes very little will receive just a little reward, but those who overcome all things will inherit all things (Rom.8:17,18; Rev.3:21; 21:7).

THE TWELVE APOSTLES: Called to Establish N.T. Church. They only had three and one- half years of training from the time of their calling to their commissioning. But those were intensified years with Jesus working with them around the clock. Jesus being with them in person teaching them by His words, life example and mighty demonstrations of His power and glory. This made it possible for them to go through God's preparative process in this abbreviated period of time. It still shows that there is a time of preparation and apprenticeship between ones calling and commissioning.

APOSTLE PAUL: Called to Reveal the Body of Christ, The Church. We have done a thorough research and study of the life and ministry of Paul. All indications are that there was a seventeen year period between his supernatural conversion and call to be an apostle and his commissioning as an apostle. He had a miraculous conversion on the road to Damascus. He was struck blind by a blinding light from God. He was led to Damascus. A disciple named Ananias received a vision from God which revealed to him where Saul/Paul was staying, what he should do for him, and what he should prophesy to him. Ananias prayed for him and Paul received his sight and was filled with the Holy Spirit. Ananias then prophesied to Paul about his apostolic calling to the Gentiles, kings and the children of Israel. Then he prophesied to Paul about the great sufferings Paul would go through for Jesus' name's sake. Paul immediately began to preach in Damascus that Jesus was the Son of God and the promised Messiah. A plot to kill him was discovered so some Christian brothers took him by night and let him down through the wall in a large basket. He went back to Jerusalem and tried to join with the apostles and disciples there but they were suspicious of him and would not believe he was a disciple of Jesus Christ.

Barnabas came to Paul's rescue by taking him to the apostles. They allowed Paul to speak, so he declared to them how he had seen the Lord on the road, that Christ Jesus had spoken to him, and how he had preached boldly in the name of Jesus. They accepted Saul as a true disciple. He preached a few times in Jerusalem and disputed with the Hellenists, but they attempted to kill him. When the brethren found out, they took Paul down to Caesarea and then sent him on to Tarsus, his hometown. He went to Arabia for three years to spend time alone with Christ Jesus. He received his revelation that Jesus was choosing Jews and Gentiles into one corporate Body of Christ, the Church. He then progressed through 14 years of making tents and preaching now and then.

Antioch, the Prophetic Activating Church. When the apostles heard that a church had started in Antioch, they sent Barnabas to find out what was happening. After Barnabas was there a short time, he left to find Paul. When he found him, he brought him back to Antioch where they ministered for a year. Then some prophets came from Jerusalem to Antioch. One of the prophets was Agabus who prophesied that there was going to be a great famine throughout the world. They took up a big offering and delegated Barnabas and Saul to take it to the brethren in Judea. After delivering the offering, they returned to Antioch and continued to work with the church. God then set things in motion to commission disciple Saul into his apostolic calling, and change his name to Paul. "Now in the church that was at Antioch there were certain prophets and teachers: Barnabas, Simeon who was called Niger, Lucius of Cyrene, Manaen who had been brought up with Herod the tetrarch, and Saul." They did not know what fivefold ministry Saul was so they mentioned all these prophets and teachers, and Saul. "As they ministered to the Lord and fasted the Holy Spirit said. 'Now separate to Me Barnabas and Saul for the work to which I have called them.'Then, having fasted and prayed, and laid hands on them, they sent them away" (Acts 13:1-3).

Prophetic Presbytery Commissioning. There were several prophets headquarted in Antioch. When Scripture states that the "Holy Spirit said." It does not mean a mighty voice thunders from heaven. It implies that one of the prophets heard the thought and intent of the Holy Spirit and verbally expressed them. We who have ministered in the prophetic for years have developed certain terminology to specify different ways that God makes known His thoughts and words. A Rhema is when an individual receives prophetic insight and divine illumination from within. When an individual prophet speaks a prophetic word we state that "the prophet spoke", or "a prophet spoke", or "Prophet Hamon prophesied." When two or more prophets prophesy to the same person, we refer to them as a "Prophetic Presbytery". After the word is confirmed and accepted as a

Holy Spirit inspired word from God then in future references to that word we normally just say "God spoke thus and so" or the "Holy Spirit said." I believe this is what Luke, the author of the book of Acts, did in writing this account. Luke recorded this incident long after it had taken place. The prophetic word spoken had already been proven to be an Holy Spirit inspired word. Without going into detail to explain how God made his thoughts known, he just wrote that "the Holy Spirit said."

A prophetic presbytery of several prophets and teachers laid hands on Barnabas and Paul, prophesied to them and gave a prophetic charge launching them into their apostolic ministry. For Paul especially this transitioned him from "called to be an apostle" to officially becoming an apostle to the gentiles with the revelation of Christ corporate church. These are some of the reasons why we call this laying on of hands anointing and prophetic activation into the apostolic ministry as a "prophetic presbytery commissioning". That is why we call Saul and Barnabas' anointing and prophetic activation into their apostolic ministry as a prophetic presbytery commissioning.

Prophets and Teachers Ministered to Apostles. It is interesting that the Holy Spirit did not speak to the apostles at Jerusalem to lay hands on and commission Paul and Barnabas to their apostolic ministry while they were there. The Holy Spirit did not choose the apostles at Jerusalem to lay hands on Paul and Barnabas and commission them to their apostolic ministry, but the Holy Spirit directed it to be done by the prophets at Antioch. Regardless of any confusion over how God made His thoughts and desires known this biblical example definitely contradicts the erroneous teaching that only apostles can commission apostles.

The Process from Calling to Commissioning Took Approximately Seventeen Years. It took seventeen years for God to feel that Saul the disciple was now ready to become Paul the Apostle of Jesus Christ and His Church. From then on they were referred to as Apostles. "But when the apostles Barnabas and Paul heard this . . . " Acts 14:14. Thus, Paul was commissioned and launched into his Apostolic ministry to the corporate Body of Christ. In the opening greetings of most of Paul's epistles, he refers to himself as an Apostle. "Paul, a servant of Jesus Christ and called to be an apostle." Rom.1:1. "Paul, called to be an apostle of Jesus Christ through the will of God." 1 Cor.1:1. "For

I speak to you Gentiles, inasmuch as I am the apostle of the Gentiles." Rom.11:13. "Whereunto I am appointed a preacher, and an apostle, and a teacher of the Gentiles." 2 Tim.1:11. "Paul, an apostle of Jesus Christ by the commandment of God our savior, and Lord Jesus Christ." I Tim. 1:1.

God's Preparation Process is for All Who are Called to be His. We have found in the Old Testament and the New Testament that God has a preparatory process for taking His chosen servants from calling to commissioning. It can be a period of time from three to thirty years. If the called one is faithful to submit to all of God's dealings and pass all the tests God gives, then the day will come when that calling becomes a commissioning. The full manifestations of that ministry will not be manifested until we progress from the state of "called to be" to fully "being" that which God chose and ordained us to be. After divine commissioning the minister should have several decades of successful ministry. Joseph had eighty years of successful ministry, David had forty, Elisha had fifty, Paul more than thirty, and Jesus Christ three and one-half years on earth and an eternal ministry as head of His Church and the universe. If we could communicate with this great cloud of witnesses concerning the value of going all the way through the process from calling to commissioning they would say, "It is worth everything you have to go through on earth to fulfill God's destiny for your lives, which results in receiving that unfathomable joy of your eternal reward in Christ Jesus." There is an old gospel hymn that expresses how we will feel on that glorious day.

> *"It will be worth it all*
> *When we see Jesus.*
> *Life's trials will seem so small*
> *When we see Christ.*
> *One glimpse of His dear face*
> *All sorrow will erase*
> *So bravely run this race*
> *Till we see Christ."*

We will find in the following chapter that God even has a process of calling to commissioning for His corporate Church. The Church was called forth on the day of Pentecost. It was birthed and seemingly grew to its apex within thirty years. It then went through its "David's Wilderness", "Joseph's Prison", "Abraham's Ishmael Ministry", and "Israel's Egyptian Bondage" for over 1000 years. The Holy Spirit was commissioned to bring full restoration to Christ's Church so that the corporate Church could be commissioned in 1500 A.D. to being fully restored and restoring all things. Finally, at Christ's second coming the Church will be launched into its eternal ministry and destiny. All conditional prophecies will have come to pass, all temporal things made eternal. All who went through God's divine process on earth until they were conformed to the image of Jesus Christ will be commissioned to their joint heir ministry with Jesus Christ. It will launch them into a successful ministry that will continue throughout the endless ages of eternity. Apostle Paul received a glimpse of eternity and exclaimed that "the sufferings in this present life are not even worthy to be compared to the glory which shall be revealed in us. To Christ be glory in the church throughout all ages, world without end. Amen" (Rom.8:18)

4

THE LAST DAY MINISTRY
OF
APOSTLES AND PROPHETS

. . . .

When the apostles are restored in their fullness, it will activate many things. It will cause many prophecies concerning the end time to start coming to pass at an accelerated rate. The apostle is the last of the fivefold ministers to be restored. It is like a great machine that needs five things to happen in sequence before it will fully work. It could be compared to space rocket boosters that must have five switches turned on before it can launch the space shuttle - the Church. Each switch or button represents one of the fivefold ministers.

The **evangelist** switch was turned on fully in the 1950's and it made progressive preparation for the launching of the Church Space Shuttle. The restoration of the **pastor** in the 1960's to his proper role did the same thing. The same with restoration of the **teacher** in the 1970's. The booster rockets turned on with all their fiery force in the 1980's with the restoration of the **prophet** and God's great company of prophets. With the full restoration of the **apostle** and God's great company of apostles the space shuttle of the Church will be launched to fulfill its end time ministry and eternal destiny.

The final restoration of apostles will cause all ministers who will receive it to be raised to a higher level of anointing and ministry. It will revolutionize the whole function of the Church. It could be compared to how the world functioned at the beginning of the twentieth century in travel, electronics and communication and how it is functioning now at the end of this century.

An Example. Just as the world went from motorized vehicles and began to fly through the air and travel into space, so will the Church advance that much in one generation. People at the turn of the twentieth century could not imagine what we would be doing by the beginning of the twenty-first century.

Only a few visionary scientists had some insight into what was coming. The common people and some leaders ridiculed their predictions. Church scientists, called prophets, have had insights and are even now having prophetic visions concerning what will be happening in the Twenty-First-Century Church. However, average saints and some church leaders deny such possibilities happening or scorn and make light of such prophetic predictions. Don't be the nearsighted and unbelieving church member, but receive the prophetic and apostolic revelations coming forth in this day and hour.

The Bible declares that natural eyes have not seen and ears have not heard all the things that God has prepared for His people. However, many of those things have already been revealed by the Holy Spirit. Isaiah and the other prophets prophesied them in the Old Testament. Paul and the other apostles wrote the revelation and applications of most of those prophecies in the New Testament. Now those things are being revealed more fully and divine applications given for appropriating and fulfilling them.

There are last day apostles and prophets that are friends of God like Prophet Abraham.

God is now revealing His plans and will continue showing them what He is about to do before He does it. Learn to recognize the true voice of God through His holy apostles and prophets (Isa. 64:4; 1Cor. 2:9,10; Eph. 3:3-5; John 15:14,15; Gen. 18:17; Isa. 41:8; Amos 3:7).

Different Types of Apostles. All the fivefold ministers - apostles, prophets, evangelists, pastors, teachers - vary in their special anointing and ability. In more than four decades of ministering with ministers around the world, I have found that most major in their God-given ascension office and minor in one of the others. For instance, there are those who are functioning as pastors but each has a different emphasis. There are pastoral pastors, apostolic pastors, prophetic pastors, evangelistic pastors and teaching pastors. It only takes being in a church one or two services to determine what type of ministry is shepherding that flock of sheep. I could give you detailed characteristics and ministry emphasis on each one. But our purpose in this book is not to explain the pastor but the apostle. The same is true for all fivefold ministers. We will use this principle to show the different types of apostles.

Apostolic-Apostles: These are the apostles whose whole ministry expression is apostolic. They are more like the Apostle Paul who demonstrated all the things that apostles are capable of being and doing. The Scriptures do not reveal that any of the original Twelve Apostles ever pastored a local church. Apostle Paul and Prophet Silas stayed two years establishing the New Testament church in Ephesus. Paul stayed eighteen months in Corinth while establishing the local church. He also stayed a few months here and there establishing churches, but he never became the long term pastor of any church.

The church world for hundreds of years has substituted the term "missionary" for the apostolic work that has been done in other nations and regions. But a true apostle is more than the typical understanding of a missionary. The Apostolic Movement will reveal and demonstrate what this type of apostle is to be and do. How he relates to local churches, how he is supported and how he relates to the other fivefold ministers and their ministries will be made known.

Prophetic-Apostles: These are true apostles but have a strong anointing for prophesying to individuals, churches and nations. They may do this as an individual minister or with others in a prophetic presbytery. Paul was a prophetic apostle. He laid hands on Timothy and prophesied to him his calling and gifts. He had the ministry of prophetically revealing things to individuals, imparting spiritual graces and gifts. (1 Tim. 4:14; 2 Tim 1:6; Rom. 1:11).

However, as an apostle he fulfilled his ministry with the discerning of spirits, faith and working of miracles. The apostolic prophet does similar things by his prophetic office gift of prophesying, the word of knowledge and gifts of healings. The end result is the same for the people but the prophet and apostle minister their anointing and ministry in a little different manner. If King David, Moses and Joseph had been active ministers in the Church, they could have been called prophetic-apostles.

Evangelistic-Apostles: These are more the missionary type. Their greatest concern is for world evangelization. If they are in a pastoral position then their church will be very outreach oriented. They will be taking teams and sending teams to the nations. They will propagate that the greatest responsibility of the apostle is reaping the harvest by mass evangelism meetings and taking the gospel to all nations.

Apostle Miracle Ministry vs. Evangelistic Miracle Ministry. We promised you in another chapter that we would show the differences between the miracle ministry of the true evangelist and that of the apostle. The basic difference is revealed in Acts the eighth chapter where an evangelistic campaign was conducted. The evangelist had one main concern, that of winning souls for Jesus Christ. Like Philip, as soon as an evangelist brings thousands to Christ in one campaign, then the Holy Spirit leads him to another evangelistic ministry whether to one or one hundred thousand.

Apostolic Miracles vs. Evangelistic Miracles. The church at Jerusalem sent Apostles Peter and John to Samaria to follow up with apostolic ministries. They established the new converts on the fundamentals of the faith, laid hands on them to receive the Holy Spirit, established them in the present-truth, ministries, and spiritual experiences of the New Testament Church Movement. They then gathered the new converts together and established them into a New Testament local church. The evangelist anointing works miracles to get them saved and then baptized in water. The apostles work miracles not only to get people saved but to establish them into a progressive growing local church. These are the main differences between the evangelistic-evangelist and the apostolic-apostle. However, there are evangelistic-apostles and apostolic-evangelists. Some who are really apostles are calling themselves evangelists, and some who are really evangelists are calling themselves apostles. They base this on the fact that they have signs, wonders and miracles following their ministry. The only way to tell the difference is by divine discernment, prophetic insight, and evaluating ones concerns and motivational purpose. Then there are those who are apostles with an evangelistic zeal who can properly be called evangelistic- apostles.

Pastoral-Apostles: Apostle James, the natural brother of Jesus, is an example of a pastoral-apostle. He pastored the local church at Jerusalem. The Bible or history does not say that he ever traveled beyond Jerusalem. He was the senior pastor of one local church during his entire ministry. He never conducted any apostolic crusades or traveled among the churches as did Peter and Paul.

James did write one letter which became The Epistle of James in the Bible. He addressed it "to the twelve tribes which are scattered abroad." The Twelve Apostles probably made Pastoral- Apostle James' local church in Jerusalem their home church when not itinerating.

Can you imagine what it would be like to have the Twelve Apostles that walked with Jesus for more than three years sitting in your congregation? Especially when you did not accept Christ as your Savior until after His resurrection. I doubt if Senior Pastor-Apostle James turned the pulpit over to one of the twelve every time they were in town.

A Modern Day Example. My thirty-eight-year-old son, Tom, who pastors our local CI Family Church has had a similar situation for the last ten years. We have twelve ministers who travel full time in ministry but make CI Family Church their home church. All eleven couples including one single are apostles, prophets, and prophetesses. Two of the men are younger than Tom, four are less than five years older and the rest are in their fifties and sixties. Jim Davis who is president of the CI Network of Churches founded a local church and pastored it for twenty years.

He is a prophetic-apostle who oversees all the CINC churches and ministers. Most of these ministers have national and international ministries. Several of them have Master's degrees and Doctorates. Pastor Tom has an Associate and Bachelor's degree and is working on his Master's.

One of the ministers who is not counted among the travelers is Tim Hamon. He is Pastor Tom's older brother, president of CI School of Theology and the CI Ministry Training College. He is an ordained minister and functions as a prophetic-teacher. Tim and five of the other ministers serve as Pastor Tom's board of elders. My wife and I, his parents, serve as bishop over the local church, over all five presidents of CI Ministries, and bishop-overseer of all CINC churches and ministries. Although I am bishop over all these ministries and have three times as much ministry experience as Tom, yet I only speak in the local church three or four times a year.

When we are home, I do not feel I have to do the preaching. I just sit on the platform with Pastors Tom and Jane and most times never say a word, but occasionally give ministry reports or a prophecy. Rarely does one of the traveling ministers have opportunity to speak on Sunday morning.

They do not come home to minister but to rest and receive personal ministry. Pastors Tom and Jane can tell you the burdens and blessings that come with pastoring a church of this nature. I'm sure if we could talk to Pastor James, he could really tell us many things about pastoring a church with many apostles, prophets and older elders of the Faith. Normally only prophetic and pastoral-apostles have the personal security, faith, grace and confidence to pastor such a church.

Teacher-Apostles: There are teaching-apostles in Bible colleges, pastoring churches and itinerating among the churches. Their greatest concern is for the establishing of saints in proper doctrine and practical living. They make volumes of outlines, teaching manuals and workbooks to help the saints be established in all truth and Christian experiences. They will make sure they have a K-12 Academy for the children, a Bible college and training programs for all groups in the church. They will have their weekly home groups organized and teaching outlines for each one to follow. They will have follow-up programs for all their converts to make sure they are firmly established in the church. Their weakness is that they have a tendency to depend on their organizational skills and programs more than their apostolic ministry for the supernatural signs, wonders and miracles.

God's supernatural power should be manifest in the apostle's ministry regardless of what type of apostle a minister may be. Apostles have been described for years as administrators, concerned about church structure, practical Christianity and ruling over others. Apostles have been so busy trying to live up to that job description until they have forsaken their greater ministry. The ministry of giving themselves to prayer, study of the word and manifesting the miraculous. It is time for all of us to make the same decision and dedication of the early church apostles. They realized they had become too involved in the administrative affairs of the church. "It is not desirable that we should leave the word of God and serve tables. Therefore . . . we will give ourselves continually to prayer and the ministry of the word." (Acts 6:2,40)

Let all fivefold ministers, and especially apostles take this biblical principle seriously. Begin now to delegate others to take care of the natural matters and many of the minor counseling and pastoral duties. Then fill up that time, not with more golfing and fishing but with hours of prayer for spiritual enlightenment while studying the word. Give yourself to activating the apostolic anointing with its divine enablement to minister with miraculous manifestations confirming the word preached. The football of obedience is now in our hands. We can either sit on it or arise and run with it toward the goal. Let us be God's type of apostle and not an apostle with some religious job description. If we older apostles do not become the Calebs and Joshuas to help lead this new generation of apostles, then God will leave us in the wilderness and raise up new leaders that are not afraid to be all that God intended for His apostles to be and manifest.

Ministries of the Last Day Apostles and Prophets. They will be the generals that lead God's fivefold officers and warrior saints into and through the final moves of God after the Apostolic Movement. Twenty years ago while prophetically writing the fifth division of the book "The Eternal Church" dealing with the future activities and destiny of the Church, the following declarations were made.

"Get Ready for New Restorational Movement"

"Oh, present generation of the Church,
especially you that are young in heart
and your eye has caught the vision and your
heart has felt the thrill,
to the call of the Master, and your heart has said,
'I will: Get ready for the conflict of the ages',
oh His fury is upon us, is upon us today."

"These are more than words to a chorus, they are the cries of the Holy Spirit to this generation. If you have never been a part of a restorational move of God, then get ready and get excited! There is another restoration truth coming to the Church that will bring us into full reality."

"But be assured it will be the same among Christendom during this time as it was when Israel was challenged to go in and possess their promised possessions. Twelve Israeli spies went into the land of Canaan. They all saw the same bountifulness and truthfulness of which God had told them about the land. But ten of them were overwhelmed with the giants, walled cities and fortified areas. Joshua and Caleb saw the impossibilities in the natural, but they believed God's prophetic promises and said, 'We are well able to overcome and possess.' The ten unbelieving spies said, 'We are not able.'" (Num. 13:30,31)

"Two Family Camps - the 'Ables' and the 'Not Ables'. This next challenge of the Holy Spirit to the Church will sound just as unreasonable, irrational, impossible, and ridiculous to the majority of present day ministers as it did to the ten natural, humanistic minded Israelis. If this Old Testament type holds true in the percentages, it means that for every two ministers who are preaching this truth there will be ten against it. Every minister in Christendom, and even those among the Charismatics, will be faced with a challenging decision. The Church will be separated into two camps; the 'we are able' group, and the 'we are not able' group. The majority has never been right. God is not looking for a multitude of leaders but for a few who are willing to cross their Jordan of death to self, arise in resurrection life and be united with the believers into a mighty army that shall go in and possess their promised possessions."

Like the prophets of old, I prophetically saw something was coming but didn't know how, when and where. I had no idea then that there would be a Prophetic Movement in the

1980's. An Apostolic Movement in the late 1990's and then three more finalizing moves of God before this came to pass in fullness. And even now I am sure there will be refreshing moves and revivals take place around these restorational moves of God. We see in part and prophesy in part but when the perfect or fullness of revelation comes then we will see the whole as God sees it from eternity.

I closed that chapter by declaring, "If I am privileged of the Holy Spirit to be a Joshua or a Caleb to this new generation, then I shall do all in my power to maintain a balance by the grace, wisdom, and maturity of the Head of the Church Himself, Jesus Christ our Lord." Thank God that 20 years later I had my first experience of being at the birthing of a sovereign restorational movement--The Prophetic Movement. As you have read in this book, I fulfilled my commitment by doing all in my power to teach, write and demonstrate God's grace, wisdom, and balance without going to extremes to the right and left. When we did make a few swings in our ignorance and enthusiasm, God quickly brought us back to the middle.

Now We Are Participating in the Apostolic Movement. If I live to the age of 85 to 90 I will probably have opportunity to be a part of the final moves of God. Several prophecies have been given to me by proven prophets and apostles that I would never miss a new move of God as long as I am alive on earth. If I leave this earth before the translation of the saints then I know I will still be a part of all that Christ Jesus will ever do throughout eternity. For I am an heir of God and joint-heir with Jesus Christ in all that He shall ever be or do in His eternal kingdom and everlasting ministry. (Rom. 8:17).

God's purpose is to use the Church to teach all earthly and heavenly creatures the manifold wisdom of God. "And to make all see what is the fellowship of the mystery, which from the beginning of the ages has been hidden in God who created all things through Jesus Christ; **to the intent** that **now** the **manifold wisdom of God might be made known by the Church** to the principalities and powers in the heavenly places, according to **the eternal purpose** which He accomplished in Christ Jesus our Lord." "Now to Him who is able to do exceedingly abundantly above all that we ask or think, according to the power that works in us, **to Him be glory in the Church** by

Christ Jesus to all generations, **forever and ever**. Amen." (Eph 3:9-11, 20, 21)

Jesus was the glory of God manifested on earth. The Church is the glory of Christ Jesus being manifested on earth. That glory will be made known by the Church throughout the endlessness of eternity. Glory means the personification of Christ's personality, portrayal of His presence, manifestation of His ministry, revelation of His reality, conveying His character, performing of His purpose, the revelation of His grace, goodness and greatness. The Church is the glory of the Lord that God shall cause to cover the earth as the waters cover the sea. (Eph. 1:12,17; 2 Cor. 3:18; Isa. 11:9; Num. 14:21; Hab. 2:14)

The Church Never Ends. It only escalates and begins on a higher realm of immortality. The corporate Body of Christ is as everlasting in its life and ministry as is Jesus Christ the Head of the Church. Membership ministry in the Body of Christ does not cease at ones death or the translation and resurrection of the Church. The Church is now and forever will be as timeless and everlasting as its God.

Some Specific Ministries of the End

Time Prophets and Apostles. As mentioned earlier they will manifest all the miracles and judgment ministries of Moses and Elijah and the two prophetic witnesses in Revelation eleventh chapter. Ministering by their anointing and the leading of the Holy Spirit, they will pronounce judgments upon the opponents of Christ and His gospel, such as Paul did by proclaiming blindness upon Elymas, the sorcerer. They will prophesy great changes in nature and the nations. They will accurately predict earthquakes, tidal waves and other catastrophes of nature. These prophecies given in the name of Jesus Christ will come to pass exactly as predicted. They will cause the fear of Jehovah God to come upon the people causing whole nations to turn to God.

New Creative Miracles in Abundance. They will produce creative miracles among the maimed and deformed. New limbs will grow back where they had been removed or never developed. Not only will there be creative miracles in the human body, there will also be creative miracles performed in nature. There will be such undeniable miracles taking place that it will shake and awake the nations (Hag.2:7).

The Gospels and the Book of Acts Reenacted. God will not do these things just to confirm someone's revelation or ministry; to satisfy curiosity or human ego, or just a desire to see the miraculous. As needs arise apostles, prophets and apostolic saints of the restored Church will do the following. They will "walk on water," be transported by the Spirit from one geographical location to another as Phillip the evangelist; multiply the loaves and fishes to feed the multitudes when there are no other resources; supernaturally preach to nationals in their own language; have supernatural preservation during calamities; be miraculously and timely directed. There will be a greater number of incidents of people being raised from the dead and many other things that would be hard now to grasp and believe they really could happen.

Church Will Reach its Peak of Performance. Jesus will continue to arise in His true present truth apostles, prophets, evangelists, pastors and teachers until the saints are perfected and moving in their ministry. Fivefold ministers will continue in their ministry to the saints until they reach Christ's fullness of maturity and ministry.

Some are even destined to "grow up into the shoulders and headship of Christ where the government of the kingdom of God will be placed upon them. The last day Church-Bride will not be a little girl [immature] or an old woman [fallen away and deteriorated] but a fully developed and grown young woman in Her prime and peak of Her performance. (Is.9:6,7; Eph.4:16)

Prerequisites for Participation in the Last Generation Church. Those who will be participants in the great apostolic and prophetic companies of overcomers will not be there simply because of their faith, revelation and preaching. They will have to be absolutely Christlike and powerful in ministry. Participants and leaders of past restorational movements were mightily used even though they were immature and carnal in areas of their lives. But those days have come to an end for the last generation who will participate in these final moves of God. The only Christians who will participate in these last activities of the mortal Church will be those who have fully died the death to sin and self. The declaration of Galatians 2:20 will have become a lifestyle reality to them. Every attitude and action contrary to divine principle will have to be purged. Nothing short of conformity to the image of Jesus Christ will suffice.

First-Century and Twenty-First Century Ministries. As the ministry of the apostle and prophet founded the Church, so shall the ministry of the apostle and prophet put the finishing touches on the Church. They are being raised up in the Church to purge the ministers and believers. There is a great lack of the reverential fear of God within Christendom. Holy Spirit baptized Christians come to church services with all types of sin in their lives. These range from sexual immorality to gossip, rebellion, selfishness and party spirits. They sing, praise, rejoice, prophesy, testify and preach as though there were nothing out of order in their lives.

Anointed ministers, especially apostles and prophets, will move into a new realm of prophecy, words of knowledge and discerning of spirits. They will openly expose this hypocrisy and cause the reverential fear of God to fall upon the congregation and preachers. The time is coming very soon when Christians will thoroughly examine themselves in prayer and the Word of God before they ever enter the doors of the local church or conference meetings. They will make sure all sin, unforgiveness and all sinfully selfish acts are fully forgiven and under the blood of Jesus. The religiously proud who try to make excuses or justify themselves by lying to the Holy Spirit who is speaking through these ministers will receive the same judgment of God as Ananias and Sapphira did when they lied to the Holy Spirit speaking through Apostle Peter. This will bring great fear and respect for the Church and God's anointed ministers. It will cause many souls to be saved and added to the Church daily. The same judgment ministry of the last day apostles and prophets will begin the greatest harvest of souls that has ever been seen during any other time of the Church Age.

The Whole Creation is Waiting for the Last Generation Church. The earth and all of creation are waiting for the manifestation of God's last day apostles and prophets and fully restored Church. "For the earnest expectation of the creation waits for the revealing of the sons of God." When the Church is fully restored then the saints will receive their final redemption, the immortalization of their mortal bodies. When this happens then the natural creation of plants and animals will be delivered from their bondage of corruption into the glorious liberty of the children of God.

We the Church have a responsibility and ministry to the rest of God's creation. The whole of creation is groaning and anxiously waiting for the Church to reach full maturity and sonship. When the Church reaches that final stage and its last act of redemption, it will cause a redemptive chain reaction throughout the heavenlies and over all the earth (Romans 8:18-23).

Another Group Waiting and Cheering Us On. There is one other group waiting for the Church to press on to the finish line. The eleventh chapter of Hebrews tells of all the great heroes of the faith. But it concludes by saying, "all these, having obtained a good testimony through faith, did not receive the promise, God having provided something better for us, that they should not be made perfect apart from us." All of those who have died in the faith since the beginning of time are cheering us on from the balcony of heaven. For they cannot be complete without the full obedience of the last generation Church.

We have come to Mount Zion, the heavenly Jerusalem and the Church of the First Born where the spirits of just saints have been made perfect but they are waiting for their final act of redemption at the first resurrection. But they cannot receive it until we, the last generation Church, fulfill our destiny. This is the reason the first two verses of chapter twelve says what we are to do because of this cloud of witnesses. When you see the word "therefore" at the beginning of a chapter read the previous verses to discover what it is "there for." "Therefore, since we are surrounded by so great a cloud of witnesses, let us lay aside every weight, and the sin which so easily ensnares us, and let us run with endurance the race that is set before us, looking unto Jesus, the author and finisher of our faith, who for the joy that was set before Him [His Church-Bride] endured the cross, despising the shame, and has sat down at the right hand of the throne of God." Father God then said to Jesus, "Sit at My right hand, Till I make Your enemies Your footstool."

God is going to make all enemies Christ's footstool and put them under His feet through Christ's corporate Body, The Church. (Hebrews 1:13; 11:39; 12:1,2, 20-22). Now accompany us on the journey to discover the final moves of God that we must experience before all these things will be accomplished.

BOOKS WRITTEN BY DR. BILL HAMON

CHURCH RESTORATION
"THE ETERNAL CHURCH"

It reveals God's eternal purpose for His Church, which is the One Universal Many-membered Corporate Body of Christ. It covers the approximate 2000 years of the Church in five areas. Its origination, deterioration, restoration and ultimate destiny. The most complete panoramic view of the Church found anywhere in print. A must for Christians to know their Christian heritage roots, present position and future ministry in ages to come.

TRILOGY OF BOOKS ON PROPHETS, PROPHETIC MOVEMENT AND MINISTRY:

1. *"PROPHETS AND PERSONAL PROPHECY"* It is the biblical manual on Prophets and prophetic ministry. Many scriptural proofs plus exciting biblical and life experiences revealing the proper guidelines for receiving, understanding and fulfilling God's personal words to individuals, churches and nations. More than 100,000 in print in six different languages.

2, *"PROPHETS AND THE PROPHETIC MOVEMENT"* A complete overview of the Prophetic Movement, its purpose and place in Church history in fulfilling God's ultimate destiny for His Church. Only in this book do you find the all important Seven Principles for determining a true restorational move of God. The ways to discern the true prophets from the false. Contrast between Church Prophets and New Agers, occultic and other false supernatural manifestations.

3. **"PROPHETS, PITFALLS & PRINCIPLES"** It reveals the pitfalls of weed seed attitudes, character flaws, and prophet syndromes found in the lives of several biblical prophets. The 10 M's for maintaining and maturing ones life and ministry are listed and explained. Answers are given to nineteen of the most common and complicated questions asked about proper principles for prophets and personal prophecy.

Major Work of over 300 pages on Apostles and the Apostolic Reformation/Movement.

"APOSTLES-PROPHETS & THE COMING MOVES OF GOD"

A full biblical and life experience coverage of Apostles, their restoration, position and colaborship with the other fivefold ministers. It contains prophetic insight concerning the three moves of God that will take place after the apostolic and before the second coming of Christ Jesus. Insight concerning times and events that are about to take place in these last days.

All of Dr. Hamon's major books listed above are taught in the Christian International Ministry Training College. CI School of Theology has written courses from these books to use in its major in the Holy Spirit and Prophetic Ministry. There are Teaching Manuals written for each book. These are great for pastors and Bible college teachers who desire to teach these subjects.

To order any of these books, teaching manuals, or courses contact Christian International by phone, letter, fax, E-Mail or Internet.

APOSTLES AND PROPHETS

THE COMING MOVES OF GOD

by Dr. Bill Hamon

. . . . .

*Foreword by **Dr. Peter Wagner***
*Endorsements by **Oral Roberts** and many others*

When apostles were active in the first generation Church, a great harvest of souls was brought in. When the apostles are fully restored, there will be the greatest harvest of souls ever. The whole world will be affected when the apostles and prophets are fully restored. Their ministries will signal the rise and fall of many nations and people. The restoration of apostles will activate the final three moves of God.

The following topics are some of the chapters in Apostles - Prophets.

Biblical perspectives of the ministry of Apostles
Apostles and church doctrine
Calling vs commissioning of Apostles and Prophets
God's desire and purpose for establishing His Church
The special ministries of apostles and prophets
The calling and ministries of fivefold ministries
Divine progressive preparation for the Apostolic Movement
Apostolic Movement and its potential extremes
Last days ministries of Apostles and Prophets
The Final moves of God
The Saints Movement
Army of the Lord and eternal judgment
The Kingdom Establishing Movement

By the time you have finished this study on God's end-time apostles and prophets, a cry will start arising within your heart for the Holy Spirit to escalate His restorational process of God's holy apostles and prophets.

CHRISTIAN INTERNATIONAL
Seminars and Ministries

SCHOOL OF THE HOLY SPIRIT
Local church Friday night meetings providing a place for prophetic ministry to the congregation and personally to individuals.

CHRISTIAN INTERNATIONAL MINISTRIES NETWORK (CIMN)
Teaching, training, and maturing prophets, prophetic ministers, a prophetic people, Apostles, and Apostolic churches.

CHRISTIAN INTERNATIONAL BUSINESS NETWORK (CIBN)
Teaching and activating Christian business people to succeed with biblical principles and prophetic perceptions, fulfilling their destiny.

PROPHETIC WORSHIP LEADERS & SONGWRITERS NETWORK
Equipping • Seminars • Networking • Tape productions

CHRISTIAN INTERNATIONAL PUBLISHERS (CIP)
Books, tapes, video's, and teaching manuals on prophetic ministry and restoration truths of the Church.

CHRISTIAN INTERNATIONAL NETWORK OF CHURCHES (CINC)
International association of Prophetic/Apostolic ministers and churches providing training and accountability based on relationship.

MINISTRY TRAINING COLLEGE (MTC)
First semester anointed biblical teaching and the second semester mentoring and training in prophetic ministry and other areas.

MANUAL FOR MINISTERING SPIRITUAL GIFTS
A 300 page manual with two 2-hour video's - 13 weekly sessions - 26 activations - Certification required. For pastors and leaders.

ORDER CI PROPHETIC MATERIALS TODAY

Books by Dr. Bill Hamon

The Eternal Church	11.95
Prophets and Personal Prophecy	10.95
Prophets and The Prophetic Movement	10.95
Prophets Pitfalls and Principles	10.95
Apostles-Prophets & The Coming Moves of God	12.95

Teaching manuals and workbooks are also available for the above mentioned books

Prophetic Destiny and The Apostolic Reformation	6.95
Fulfilling Your Personal Prophecy	3.95

Books by Evelyn Hamon

The Spiritual Seasons of Life	3.95

Audio Teaching Tape Series

Prophetic Pitfalls (Dr. Bill Hamon)	30.00
The 10 M's (Dr. Bill Hamon)	15.00
Plugging Into Your Gifts (Dr. Bill Hamon and others)	30.00
Handling Life's Realities (Evelyn Hamon)	20.00
Dealing With Life's Challenges (Evelyn Hamon)	20.00

Prophetic Praises Cassette Tapes & CDs

Mighty Man of War	Tape: 9.95
Roar, Lion of Judah	Tape: 9.95
The God of Glory Thunders	Tape: 9.95
Lord Sabaoth	Tape: 9.95
The Shout of a King	Tape: 9.95
	CD: 14.95
Fan the Flame	Tape: 9.95
	CD: 14.95

Lead sheets, sound tracks, and computer disks are available for each title

Other Materials

Manual for Ministering Spiritual Gifts - by Certificaiton only
Many more audio, video, and books available

Special 15% discount when your order is over $30.00

To order call: **1-800-388-5308**

Have your MasterCard, VISA or AMEX ready when you call!

or write: **CHRISTIAN INTERNATIONAL**
P.O. Box 9000, Santa Rosa Beach, FL 32459

Shipping costs: (based on retail value) $3.50 to $30.00=$3.00. More than
$30.00=10% of retail value. *Outside US:* 15% or retail order ($5.00 minimum)
for regular surface mail. Contact shipping for exact costs of Airmail.
Prices subject to change without notice.